S·H·P

THE
SCHOOLS
HISTORY
PROJECT

CW00672019

DISCOVERING THE PAST

SPECIAL NEEDS SUPPORT MATERIALS

MEDIEVAL REALMS

TEACHERS' RESOURCE BOOK

COLIN SHEPHARD   ANN MOORE

JOHN MURRAY

The authors and publishers would like to thank all the schools which trialled these materials, and in particular to thank Barbara Brown, teacher adviser for special educational needs in Warwickshire, for her helpful advice and comments.

Photographs are reproduced by courtesy of the British Library (cover), Cambridge University Collection (p.88) and Peter Dunn/English Heritage (p.108).

Illustrations by David Anstey, Art Construction, Sarah Blair, Ann Moore and Chris Mutter

Layouts by Amanda Hawkes

Printed and bound in Great Britain by St Edmundsbury Press, Bury St Edmunds

A CIP catalogue record for this book is available from the British Library

ISBN 0-7195-5381-4

Contrasts and Connections Pupils' Book ISBN 0-7195-4938-8
   Teachers' Resource Book ISBN 0-7195-4962-0
Discovering Medieval Realms Pupils' Book ISBN 0-7195-5177-3
   Teachers' Evaluation Pack ISBN 0-7195-5178-1
Medieval Realms Special Needs Support Materials
   Picture Pack ISBN 0-7195-5382-2
   Teachers' Resource Book ISBN 0-7195-5381-4

THE SCHOOLS HISTORY PROJECT

This project was set up by the Schools Council in 1972. Its main aim was to suggest suitable objectives for history teachers, and to promote the use of appropriate materials and teaching methods for their realization. This involved a reconsideration of the nature of history and its relevance in secondary schools, the design of a syllabus framework which shows the uses of history in the teaching of adolescents, and the setting up of appropriate examinations.

Since 1978 the project has been based at Trinity and All Saints' College, Leeds. It is now self-funding and with the advent of the National Curriculum it has expanded its publications to provide courses throughout Key Stages 1–3, and for a range of GCSE and A level syllabuses. The project provides INSET for all aspects of National Curriculum, GCSE and A level history, and also publishes *Discoveries*, a twice-yearly journal for history teachers.

Enquiries about the project, INSET and *Discoveries* should be addressed to the Schools History Project, Trinity and All Saints' College, Brownberrie Lane, Horsforth, Leeds LS18 5HD.

Enquiries about the *Discovering the Past* series should be addressed to the publishers, John Murray.

Series consultants
Terry Fiehn
Tim Lomas
Martin and Jenny Tucker

Contents

Introduction

All too often the history diet offered to pupils with special needs has consisted of crosswords, word-searches and 'gap-filling'. SHP's special needs support materials, on the other hand, have been developed to meet a specific demand from schools for materials that have all the hallmarks of SHP's 'real history' approach – in which pupils investigate issues and explore sources for themselves, and reach their own conclusions – but which at the same time recognise the very real problems some pupils have with the language of written source material and the unstructured nature of some historical tasks.

SHP's **Medieval Realms** unit was awarded the coveted TES Textbook Award in 1993. It is not only one of the best selling books on this unit but is also widely recognised as one of the most challenging and rewarding approaches to the subject. The hope is that these materials will make the unit accessible to a still wider range of pupils.

These materials have been developed by a team of writers and special needs advisers. They have also been trialled in a number of schools around the country. The result is a set of flexible and innovative strategies which aim to:
- motivate pupils to find out about medieval Britain, by developing their historical skills and understanding at an appropriate level
- give all pupils access to this important core unit
- add variety to the teaching of Medieval Realms.

The materials consist of this Teachers' Resource Book, with more than 200 largely photocopiable pages, and a companion Picture Pack, which contains 23 full-colour, large-size pictorial sources, together with a wide range of suggested activities using the pictures. All in all these materials provide several 'pathways' through Medieval Realms which will suit a wide range of classroom situations.

The three pathways

- Pathway 1 is for pupils who have severe difficulties with reading. Through the Picture Pack they can receive a 'minimum entitlement' **Medieval Realms** unit – through the use of pictorial source material alone.
- Pathway 2 is for lower-ability pupils who can, nonetheless, cope with a certain amount of carefully targeted reading and writing. The Picture Pack and the differentiated worksheets, games and stories in this accompanying Teachers' Resource Book together provide a flexible alternative to using a class textbook. Indeed, this pathway can operate independently of any textbook and does not require users to have classroom sets of SHP's **Medieval Realms** unit.
- Pathway 3. In classes where SHP's *Contrasts and Connections* or *Discovering Medieval Realms* is being used as the classroom textbook, the Picture Pack and the Teachers' Resource Book provide a wide range of materials to support slower learners and reluctant readers, by simplifying written source material and giving structure for pupils' written responses to questions in the textbook.

Main features of the support materials

These support materials respond to a number of the important requirements of low-attaining pupils:

Motivation

- In common with the entire *Discovering the Past* series, the main aim of the support materials is to help pupils of all abilities to realise how fascinating history can be and to enjoy participating in history lessons.
- The course is founded on the belief that pupils of all abilities can cope with investigation of real historical issues *as long as they are presented at an appropriate level*.
- The materials aim to give pupils a high success rate – to increase motivation by ensuring positive achievement.

Differentiation

- While the materials in SHP's **Medieval Realms** unit are demonstrably capable of differentiation 'by outcome', there is often a need to differentiate 'by task'. Used alongside the core unit, these materials vastly increase the opportunities for differentiating pupils' work in Y7. The detailed teachers' notes which follow indicate many ways in which further differentiation can be achieved.

General learning skills

- The materials encourage a variety of methods of learning.
- They also aim to involve pupils in decisions about their learning, making them aware of the learning objectives and helping them to recognise what progress they are making.

Minimum entitlement

- The authors have defined a minimum entitlement for **Medieval Realms** with three main focus points: 'The Norman Conquest', 'Life in a medieval village', and 'Problems facing medieval kings'.

Language skills

- The support materials have not been written to a single formula – nor have they been written at a single level. Instead, the language level of the authors' text, the written sources and the tasks has been carefully monitored to ensure it is totally suited to the *nature of the material* and the *learning context* of the pupils. For example, in certain tasks where group learning is being encouraged and pupils can gain support from their peers, a higher level of language is deemed appropriate than where pupils are working independently.

■ The materials are designed to complement the language policy of the school in a number of ways:
- by enhancing pupils' general reading skills
- by developing pupils' subject-specific vocabulary (through the use of a feature called 'History Dictionary')
- by developing higher-order reading skills, such as text interrogation and cross-referencing skills
- by ensuring that pupils' writing tasks are always undertaken for a purpose and for a good range of purposes
- by providing plentiful opportunities for group discussion.

Using these support materials

In this book you will find more than 150 photocopiable worksheets which focus on key aspects of the **Medieval Realms** programme of study, in particular:
■ the Battle of Hastings and the Norman Conquest (Sections 2 and 3; Tasks 9–23)
■ life in a medieval village (Sections 4–8; Tasks 24–49)
■ problems facing medieval kings (Sections 9–11; Tasks 50–57).

Planning your course

There are two main ways to use these materials.

1. They can be used as a self-standing course. We have covered the main areas of the programme of study for **Medieval Realms** and all the key elements of the unit. The activities are self-contained in that all the sources and resources you need to run the activities are provided for you in the Teachers' Resource Book and in the companion Picture Pack. There is no requirement that you have stocks of *Contrasts and Connections*, *Discovering Medieval Realms* or any other textbook. These materials can provide you with a worksheet-based course which can be used alongside any textbook or none.

2. They can equally well be used to support the use of SHP's **Medieval Realms** unit in schools which are already using *Contrasts and Connections* or *Discovering Medieval Realms*. The aim has been to make selected enquiries more accessible to those with learning difficulties. This has been achieved by:
■ giving additional structure for pupils' tasks
■ narrowing the selection of source material for pupils to work with
■ further simplifying the language of the written sources
■ providing much bigger visuals for the pupils to work with (in the Picture Pack)
■ helping teachers to identify where pupils need help in making progress in history.

This book provides differentiated materials which enable pupils with learning difficulties to examine the same issues and tackle the same enquiries as mainstream pupils using *Contrasts and Connections*. It allows them to develop their understanding of the same historical concepts as the rest of the class, but at their own pace and to their own level. And as their understanding grows, some pupils will be able to move confidently from support materials to textbook – choosing to work on the tasks in *Contrasts and Connections* in preference to the tasks in this book.

Trialling experience has shown that in practice these materials are immensely flexible and that they can also provide invaluable support for pupils of a much wider range of abilities than simply those with learning difficulties. In some schools, exercises such as those based on the Black Death story, 'Alice's Wedding Day' (Task 38), or the Battle of Hastings sequence cards in Task 11, have proved useful as a starting point for entire classes, leading them into the relevant enquiries in *Contrasts and Connections*.

Differentiation

Differentiation is about helping pupils to progress at their own speed – hardly a novel idea. Yet the word sometimes fills people with fear, maybe because it has become the focus of recent criticism by OFSTED inspectors.

The problem is, of course, that all pupils are different, yet are usually taught together in groups of about thirty. How can teachers help each of them to progress at his/her own pace? These materials will offer you a practical set of strategies for achieving differentiation in your history teaching. However, some preliminary words of caution are needed. Discussion about differentiation is too often hampered by the assumption that it simply involves giving pupils different work to do. This obscures the fact that if pupils are to make progress then some more basic aspects of good practice are important. These following aspects of good practice have formed the bedrock of the strategies in the support materials:

1. Making aims and objectives clear We have tried to set clear aims and objectives and to help pupils understand what these are. The detailed notes which follow describe the aims of each task. We would encourage you always to talk with pupils about what is being done and why. This applies both on the overall level of planning a route through the unit (see Task 8), and at the level of the individual exercise.

2. Making objectives achievable We have tried to ensure that these tasks can be tackled at a range of levels. Only you will know what is really achievable with your individual pupils – so we have tried to give you plenty of opportunities to set specific, itemised, achievable objectives for each pupil, for example 'to find out four things about

A sample worksheet

Header shows the number of worksheet pages needed to do this task, and 'You will need' lists other materials pupils will need to complete the activity. These features help put pupils more effectively in control of their own learning.

'History Dictionary' box Whenever necessary this box provides the support which pupils need in order to understand subject-specific vocabulary *before* they meet the word in the worksheet. You can, if you wish, add other words to the History Dictionary box before you make photocopies. The use of this feature is explained on page 15.

Introductory text This is kept to the minimum necessary to introduce the task. Further background information and help with contextualising the task are provided in the detailed teachers' notes (pages 17–30) for you to use if you think it necessary.

Worksheet title

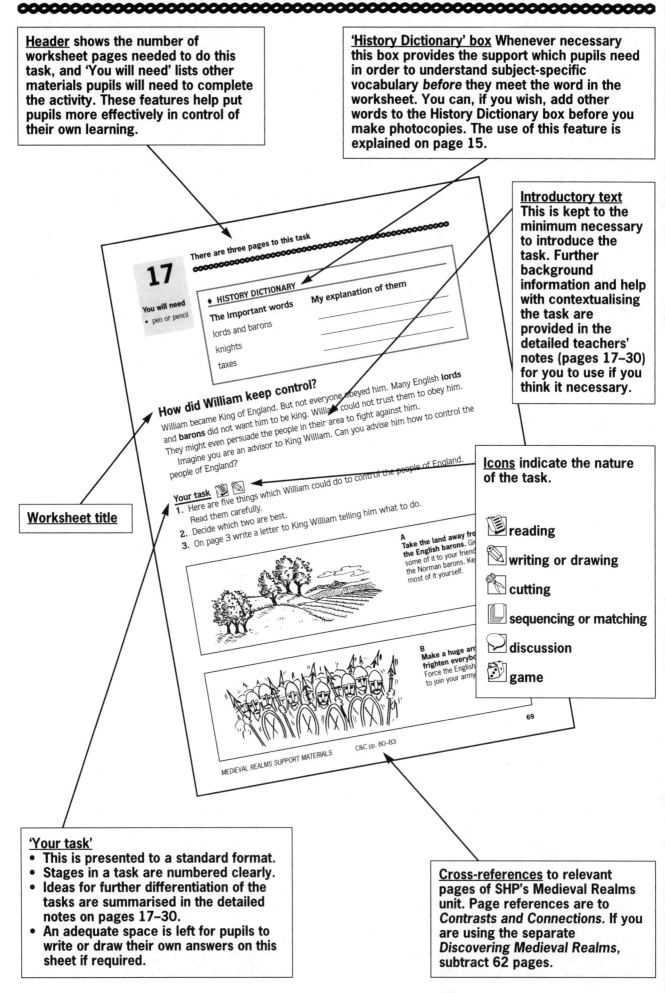

17

You will need
• pen or pencil

There are three pages to this task

◆ HISTORY DICTIONARY
The important words   My explanation of them
lords and barons
knights
taxes

How did William keep control?

William became King of England. But not everyone obeyed him. Many English **lords** and **barons** did not want him to be king. William could not trust them to obey him. They might even persuade the people in their area to fight against him.
Imagine you are an advisor to King William. Can you advise him how to control the people of England?

Your task
1. Here are five things which William could do to control the people of England. Read them carefully. Decide which two are best.
2. Decide which two are best.
3. On page 3 write a letter to King William telling him what to do.

A
Take the land away fro
the English barons. Giv
some of it to your friend
the Norman barons. Ke
most of it yourself.

B
Make a huge ar
frighten everybo
Force the English
to join your army

69

MEDIEVAL REALMS SUPPORT MATERIALS   C&C pp. 80–83

Icons indicate the nature of the task.

   reading

   writing or drawing

   cutting

   sequencing or matching

   discussion

   game

'Your task'
• This is presented to a standard format.
• Stages in a task are numbered clearly.
• Ideas for further differentiation of the tasks are summarised in the detailed notes on pages 17–30.
• An adequate space is left for pupils to write or draw their own answers on this sheet if required.

Cross-references to relevant pages of SHP's Medieval Realms unit. Page references are to *Contrasts and Connections*. If you are using the separate *Discovering Medieval Realms*, subtract 62 pages.

medieval villages'. (See also the notes on the Special Needs Code of Practice on page 8.)

3. <u>Monitoring and assessing the progress the pupils are making</u> If pupils are to make progress, formative assessment is essential and these materials offer plentiful opportunity for you to make your own written, narrative comments on pupils' work. These comments should identify and praise achievement but also provide signposts for future work. Talking with pupils about their work and encouraging self-assessment – by allowing them to select pieces of their own work to display in a portfolio – is an effective way of encouraging progress.

4. <u>Building on what the pupils already understand and re-applying skills and understanding in a new context</u> In rough terms about 80 per cent of what takes place in a lesson should be consolidating what has already been achieved in terms of skills and understanding. About 20 per cent should involve setting pupils new challenges or introducing new ideas. If you go any faster you will risk losing many pupils; if you go more slowly, they may be bored through a lack of challenge. Throughout this material we have therefore introduced new content and ideas gradually, step-by-step, and offered regular opportunities for pupils to revisit skills and concepts in a new context.

5. <u>Using a variety of teaching and learning styles</u> Pupils are best motivated by the use of a range of learning situations and teaching methods. These materials can give them the experience of whole class work, small group work, work in pairs and individual work. There are opportunities for discussion as well as writing, drawing, matching, sequencing and source interrogation. One should not underestimate the power of the well-told story in history teaching. There is therefore also a small number of stories which forms the backbone of pupils' work on the medieval village, the Black Death, and life in towns.

6. <u>Encouraging pupils to experiment and take risks</u> We have avoided activities which deal mostly in 'right and wrong' answers. They lead to pupils becoming discouraged. They will avoid participating because of the fear of making mistakes. We have preferred to use open questions and problem-solving enquiries where all genuine efforts can be praised. By encouraging group work and allowing pupils to work in small groups with others of similar ability it should be possible, with careful planning, for each pupil to make a valuable contribution to the overall group effort.

The most essential factor in differentiation remains <u>the role of the teacher in the classroom</u>. Many teachers will offer appropriate support to pupils of different abilities as a matter of course. This can take various forms. It is worth your considering how effectively this is done in your own department. Teachers will often rephrase explanations and instructions for the whole class. Extra explanation and support will be given to individual pupils as the teacher walks around the classroom discussing the work. During these discussions teachers might provide more structure for some pupils or reduce the demands by helping with the first few steps of the work. They might point individual pupils towards other resources which will help them with their work.

There will never be just one correct approach to differentiation, and effective differentiation cannot be achieved overnight. You will constantly need to adapt and adjust your teaching methods and your presentation of activities to allow individual pupils to progress. The bulk of the detailed notes is concerned with the matter of how to achieve further differentiation for individual pupils by varying the input and support given, by providing additional structure for an answer, and by asking pupils to respond in different ways.

Classroom management

If you are using these materials alongside *Contrasts and Connections*, there are specific issues of classroom management to be addressed. How can the use of these materials dovetail into the use of the textbook? In particular, how can you use them with a small number of pupils in a class that is using a textbook? Of course there is no 'blueprint' for this. Because these materials are deliberately flexible you must find your own way through and adapt them where necessary. However, here are three examples which show the material in use:

<u>Example 1</u> A Y7 mixed-ability class is preparing to study the Battle of Hastings. The whole class is using pages 68–69 of *Contrasts and Connections*. The teacher has told the pupils the story in the first four paragraphs on page 68. Most pupils then tackle the 'yellow-box' questions on page 69 which demand detailed work on sources from the Bayeux Tapestry.

The pupils then have a choice. To look at why the Battle of Hastings happened they can go on to study pages 70–75 of *Contrasts* which lay out the background (the claims to the throne and the preparation for the battle) in some detail, <u>or</u> they can use Task 9 (which summarises the information on pages 70–73 of *Contrasts*) and Tasks 10 and 11 in the support materials, which concentrate simply on establishing a sequence for the events which lead to the battle.

Some pupils might opt for the former pathway but then, finding it too difficult, decide to change to the alternative. Others might switch route, but in the opposite direction.

Whichever pathway has been taken, however, all the class can then tackle Task 12 on the causes of the Battle of Hastings. This task provides a structure for a piece of extended writing which can be completed (albeit at different levels of complexity) by pupils who have been tackling *Contrasts and Connections* (pages 70–75) and by pupils who have been tackling Tasks 9–11.

Example 2 A Y7 mixed-ability class is preparing to investigate life in medieval villages. The teacher gives each pupil a copy of the story 'Alice's Unhappy Day' (Task 25). The pupils read this in small groups.

Some groups will complete this quickly, and go on to use pages 84–85 of *Contrasts* together with Tasks 24 or 27 of the support materials as homework.

Other groups will read the story more slowly. They will need support from the teacher as they mark on a plan of the village the places Alice visited and then tackle Task 26. This group might do no more work on Wharram Percy or on archaeology – the Alice story serves only to give them a flavour of village life, as a prelude to their work on another village, Elton.

Example 3 A Y7 mixed-ability class is studying the Peasants' Revolt using *Contrasts and Connections*. They are all tackling Source 1 on page 140. The pupils are given the choice of using the written version and tackling the yellow-box questions beneath it, or using the simplified and illustrated version in Task 57 and the map/sequencing task provided there.

The Code of practice on Special Educational Needs

Working together to enable children with a range of needs to learn effectively has always been recognised as good educational practice. 'It presents teachers with some of the most challenging and rewarding work the education service can offer.' *(Code of Practice on Special Educational Needs 1994)*

Every school's special needs policy now reflects the 'Staged Response to Learning Needs' which was outlined in the 1994 Code of Practice, and all teachers are expected to demonstrate how they differentiate children's learning experiences to meet these needs. The **Medieval Realms** support materials have been written to enable teachers to plan learning experiences which cover a wide range of learning needs and which can link both directly and indirectly with the core textbook.

Planning for Stage 1 of the 'Staged Response to Learning Needs'

There are several stages of learning need for which teachers now have to plan (see fig. 1). Most children with special needs are within the first stage. Their understanding and enjoyment of history will grow through using the **Medieval Realms** support materials as a stimulus for more in-depth work from a textbook (whichever this may be). They will also make progress as a result of the time teachers always invest in quality discussion and explanation with children who are learning more slowly.

When planning history for these children, teachers will be able to use their normal schemes of work, highlighting or underlining the planned activities and resources which have been differentiated for those children within Stage 1. The sample planner and blank matrix on pages 10 and 11 will be useful tools in such planning. Teachers could also record in their class register which children fall into this category so that it is clear at whom the differentiated planning has been targeted.

Planning for Stages 2 and 3

For those children whose learning needs are more complex and who fall within Stages 2 and 3, planning, monitoring and evaluation intensify. The Special Needs Co-ordinator and possibly the Support Services will be involved. The **Medieval Realms** materials have been designed to present achievable targets for these children too as the planning matrix on the following page demonstrates. The matrix enables teachers to set targets for pupils who have been identified as having general learning difficulties. These targets would normally be agreed upon with the Special Needs Co-ordinator, the support teacher and, where appropriate, the child him/herself. The targets for Stages 2 and 3 are a focus of particular attention at OFSTED inspections.

Children's individual entitlement

We are all aware that learning does not always progress in a clear linear fashion, and children do not always remain conveniently within the stages provided by the Code of Practice! However, these support materials, in defining the minimum entitlement for each topic, and in providing differentiated tasks, provide a framework within which children can progress at a rate which suits their individual learning needs.

Stage 1:	**Class or subject teachers** identify or register a child's special educational needs and, consulting the school's SEN Co-ordinator, take initial action.
Stage 2:	The school's **SEN Co-ordinator** takes the lead responsibility for gathering information and for co-ordinating the child's special educational provision, working with the child's teachers.
Stage 3:	Teachers and the SEN Co-ordinator are supported by **specialists from outside the school.**
Stage 4:	**The LEA** considers the need for a statutory assessment and, if appropriate, makes a multidisciplinary assessment.
Stage 5:	**The LEA** considers the need for a statement of special educational needs and, if appropriate, makes a statement and arranges, monitors and reviews provision.

Schools and LEAs will need to be able to demonstrate, in their arrangements for children with special educational needs, that they are fulfilling their statutory duty to have regard for this code. In the case of schools, OFSTED and OHMCI(Wales) inspection teams will consider the effectiveness of schools' policies and practices and the extent to which schools have had regard for the code.

Fig. 1 Stages of Provision

EXAMPLE

Year 7 History Unit: Medieval Realms

Names of Pupils

....

....

General target

To increase the time spent on the task, encourage pupils to collaborate with others and to develop responsibility for their own learning.

Support planned

Special Support Assistant working with two pupils, one at Stage 2 and one at Stage 3. Pupils to be encouraged to locate their own resources. Direction and intervention to be minimal. Support to concentrate on questioning and discussion. Observations on how children are approaching task to be discussed after the lesson.

Specific target for this lesson

To examine a representation of character through a picture (Stages 2 and 3), and to compare two interpretations (Stage 2).

content	vocabulary	key questions	historical skills and concepts	teaching and learning activity	resources
King John	barons priests	How did the artist make King John seem good? Why did some people have a different impression of King John?	Use and interpretation of sources	_Stages 2 and 3_ Use colour pictorial source from _Contrasts_ or outline from support materials. Discuss with children what they think of the picture. Does King John look kind? Point out facial expression, the setting and the dog. Children work in pairs, circling the items on the line drawing which give a good impression of King John. _Stage 2_ Present one contrasting written source. Discussion with children as to how it is different. Children amend an outline drawing of King John to reflect the sentiments in the written source.	(Colour pictorial source from _Contrasts_ p.135) Outline drawing from support materials Written source from support materials

Year: History   Unit:

Names of Pupils	Support planned
....	

General target	Specific target for this lesson

content	vocabulary	key questions	historical skills and concepts	teachers and learning activity	resources

MEDIEVAL REALMS

stick a picture here

Name _____ **Class** _____

Year _____ **School** _____

Name _____

Date _____

Topic _____

Name _____

Date _____

Topic _____

_____

_____

_____

_____

_____

_____

_____

_____

_____

_____

_____

_____

_____

_____

_____

Practical considerations

Preparation

Many of the tasks do require a certain amount of preparation. We have attempted to highlight in the detailed notes where there is a particular need for this. However, here are a few general points to bear in mind.

For activities such as Task 6 or 11 you can enlarge pictures, captions and text before cutting them out. Mounting these on thin card and laminating them extends their shelf life and means less preparation the following year!

There are some 'resource sheets' – e.g. good news and bad news cards for Task 46 – which need copying on to different-coloured card.

Most of the tasks have more than one page. You can give the sheets out one by one. Occasionally the later sheets in the task are 'extension sheets' only, to be available if a pupil asks for them.

If you are planning to use the 'History Dictionary' feature, you will need to photocopy the definitions on pages 203–208 on to card.

The teaching environment

Don't forget how much the teaching environment can help pupils. The walls of the classroom are a potential resource if you cover them with helpful illustrations, charts, diagrams and timelines to which pupils can refer.

Reference material (e.g. the History Dictionary file – see below) should be readily available.

A pupil folder

There are obvious benefits in pupils creating a **Medieval Realms** folder in which to store their completed drawings, written answers, worksheets, and their larger pieces of work.

To give extra coherence and status to this file, there is a photocopiable 'title page' for pupils to personalise for the front of their folders (see page 12).

There are also two matching photocopiable templates (lined for written work and unlined for artwork) both with attractive 'medieval' borders, and spaces for pupils to write in their names, the date and the topic. Hopefully these will encourage pupils to take a pride in their work. You will find these templates on pages 13 and 14 of this book.

Teachers could encourage pupils to think in terms of constructing their own history book.

'My route through *Medieval Realms*'

An important part of ensuring motivation is setting appropriate achievable targets and allowing pupils to monitor their own progress against these targets (see above under 'Differentiation'). The photocopiable planning sheet in task 8 is designed to help teacher and pupil plan together and record progress. This can also be added to the pupil's folder of work.

Timelines

All pupils need a chronological framework, not just those with learning difficulties. It would be useful to have the following two timelines prepared:

1. A horizontal timeline spanning around 5000 years, with the names of different eras, and in relevant sections dating by centuries. You could use frieze paper or wallpaper for this.

Whenever pupils are being introduced to a new study unit or are revising their skills of chronology, they should look at this timeline. It is important that they are helped to gradually develop an understanding of where, in general terms, **Medieval Realms** stands in relation to. e.g., **The Roman Empire** or **The Making of the UK.**

2. The other timeline should be for the period the class is studying; in this case the Middle Ages. This should be on as large a scale as possible – dating by decades is ideal. The timeline could be mounted on sugar paper or wallpaper lining and pinned to the wall.

As well as dates, give it shape by adding kings/queens and pictures of the main events.

Pupils can add to the timeline as their knowledge and understanding of the period increase.

Sometimes it is useful to divide the timeline up into parallel sections – one row each for political, social, economic and cultural developments. Each section can be colour-coded and added to as and when the need arises.

The History Dictionary

Throughout their study of history, pupils will come across strange and unfamiliar vocabulary. One recommendation of this course is that pupils compile their own history dictionary. They could do the same for each study unit.

This dictionary can be either a small (indexed) book – such as you can buy very cheaply in a stationer's – or it can be a set of sheets in the back of pupils' **Medieval Realms** folders.

The dictionary should include not only concepts relating to the period, e.g. baron, peasant, but also explanations of unfamiliar concepts such as 'conquest' or 'invasion' which appear across a number of units.

Each pupil's dictionary should also have explanations of key methodological words such as 'historical source', 'evidence' and 'chronology'.

Pupils can add other words to their 'History Dictionary' if they wish. Some may choose to make quite an extensive list.

Each time pupils come across an unknown or important new word, they should be encouraged to record it in their own dictionary – and they can also illustrate it if they wish.

Throughout the tasks in this book, new words are introduced and explained. The key ones are included in a History Dictionary box at the head of the worksheet. A definition can be given by the teacher or worked out by the pupil. Teachers should remind pupils to transfer these words and concepts into their own 'History Dictionaries'. Wherever possible we have deliberately tried to leave space in the box so that you can add other words which you think your pupils will have trouble with before you copy the worksheet.

To help pupils who wish to write their own definitions, we have provided a photocopiable set of definitions of the key terms (pages 203–208). These can be photocopied on to card and kept available in a file in the classroom for pupils to consult when they are writing their definitions.

The dictionary definitions can also be used in other ways. For example, you can give pupils two or three definitions and ask them to find pictorial sources in the textbook or in the Picture Pack to illustrate them.

The Picture Pack

The Picture Pack forms an essential part of this bank of resources. It contains 23 full-colour, laminated images at large size, chosen from *Contrasts and Connections*.

Experience has shown that some pupils find it easier still to work with black outline drawings of these sources – particularly because these can simplify some of the detail of the original image, and be used for pupils to label and mark. Black outlines of some images have been included on the worksheet pages themselves (e.g. Tasks 5 and 34). For further flexibility, black outlines of all 23 images can be found on pages 209–24 of this book.

Detailed teachers' notes

The aims of the detailed notes which follow are:
■ to summarise the aims of each activity
■ to highlight any preparation that may be necessary
■ to suggest how to use the activities to maximum effect in the classroom, and in particular to indicate links with SHP's **Medieval Realms** unit
■ to suggest how further differentiation can be achieved by adjusting the way in which the task is presented. Some of the suggestions for differentiation will, we hope, stretch the more able, whilst others will allow still greater access for the least able.

To indicate which way the extension lies, we have used symbols as follows:

 upward extension which makes the task more challenging for pupils who are improving more rapidly

an even more challenging activity

an alternative approach to the activity which we think is neither easier nor more difficult than the task we have set, but simply allows for a variety of teaching styles

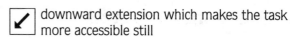 downward extension which makes the task more accessible still

a task which should be accessible to the least able

Teachers' notes

Section 1: Introduction

Aims

Tasks 1–5 might be called 'foundation strategies'. They focus on two key areas of historical understanding as well as introducing **Medieval Realms**:

1. Chronology – Tasks 1–3 help pupils develop their map of the past, and in particular to see where the Middle Ages fit into it.
2. Sources – Tasks 4–5 introduce pupils to the kind of sources we have available to us as evidence about the Middle Ages.

Tasks 6–8 then lay out some basic building blocks for understanding medieval society.

Task 1: What is history?

Aim: for pupils to identify some important events in their past

Introduction: This task should be a whole class activity, probably best used as the basis for class discussion.

Before pupils are given the worksheet, discuss with them the question 'What do you think history is?' Write the results of the discussion on the board.

Then compare the class definition to the one we have provided on the sheet. Discuss which is better. Which do the class prefer?

In their folders, pupils write down either
a) their own definition
b) the book definition
c) the class definition.

↔ Pupils copy the definition 'History is all about what people did in the past' on to a piece of paper. They are given a drawing of Harold being killed. They stick it underneath their definition, then
i) colour in the man they think is being killed
ii) write down what they think is happening in the picture.

↗ Pupils think of famous events in history. They write them down on pieces of card. The cards are pegged on to a washing line hung across the classroom. Homework activity is to find out yet more events. These are added to the line (in chronological order, of course!)

Important events in the past: Ask a volunteer to recount in detail what he or she did that morning. Ask another volunteer to do the same for the previous weekend, and so on back to last Christmas and then this time last year.

The further back into the past we go, the more difficult it is to remember what happened. Why do they think this is? Is it only the **important** things which are remembered?

Discuss with them: 'If as historians we only want to record the important things, how do we decide what to record and what to discard?'

↔ As an alternative to looking at the list of important events of the author's past, you, the teacher, could recount some important events of **your** past before pupils make the lists for their own lives.

Task 2: Putting events into chronological order

Aim: for pupils to see the purpose and the use of a timeline

Your task: Page 2 should be copied twice per pupil, cut and pasted to make a horizontal timeline.

Task 3: Putting periods of history into chronological order

Aim: for pupils to see that historians break history up into periods of time and to see whereabouts in history the Middle Ages fit

Introduction: Bring out a large roll-out 5000-year timeline (see general notes about timelines on page 15). Point out on it the period of the Romans. Ask some pupils to go and stand where they think the Stone Age was in relation to the timeline.

Your task: It would be best for pupils to work in groups. When they have matched all the cards, they stick the pairs on to a long horizontal timeline.

✓ Start with only three pairs and gradually add the others.

↗ Pupils can go to the class supply of textbooks and find a picture to go with each period.

↗ Pupils find out what BC and AD mean. They try to come up with definitions for their history dictionary.

Task 4: How we find out about the past: historical sources

Aim: for pupils to appreciate that sources can help us find out about our own past *and* about other episodes of history

Introduction:
1. Start with a class discussion.
Who can pupils talk to about their past? Who did they talk to to complete the exercise in Task 2?
Have any of them been in hospital? What record of their stay do they have?
2. Alternatively bring in your own collection of memorabilia and use it as a basis for discussion. Perhaps introduce the word 'artefact' if you think it appropriate. You can have great fun, but be doing some useful work, by setting out the artefacts in a row and asking pupils what each artefact was used for. Even artefacts from just 10 or 20 years ago can be strange to children of today. Class brainstorm about different types of historical sources. As a follow-up pupils could bring in an object each and talk about its usefulness as a source for their past.

↗ Pupils draw one of teacher's or classmate's artefacts. Make deductions as to what it tells them about the teacher/classmate.

Task 5: Using historical sources to find out about the Middle Ages

(*C&C* pp.64–65)

Aim: for pupils to use two contrasting historical sources as evidence about the Middle Ages and to summarise the impressions each source gives of the period

This covers similar ground to *Contrasts* pages 64–65, but by using only two images it simplifies the task considerably. N.B. Both images are also available in the Picture Pack. Pupils can also mark and label the black and white outlines on pages 211 and 221.

Question 2: This unstructured question is designed to provide progression from question 1, but if that is inappropriate you could give descriptions to match up with letters as we have done for question 1.

(page 4)
This is extension material for users of *Contrasts and Connections*. If you are not using *Contrasts*, still talk through the text and questions at the bottom of page 4 with the pupils after they have considered question 3.

Task 6: What kind of people lived in the Middle Ages?

Aim: for pupils to be introduced to eight different characters or types whom they will meeting through this unit, and to realise that people varied in terms of wealth and power in the Middle Ages

Preparation: Enlarge the drawings to A3 size if possible.

Your task:

Give pupils only two people: the king and the peasant. Introduce the others at a later date.

For Question 6 pupils could be asked what they think is missing from each picture **before** they see the clothing and equipment on page 4.

Also for question 6 they could add the missing parts and then compare their finished product with the symbols in the matrix.

(page 5)
This should be a discussion-based exercise. Pupils should certainly not attempt it cold. However, they can use the worksheet to record their answers once discussion has clarified the issues involved.

(page 6)
Introduction: Discuss with pupils who is rich and powerful today and perhaps make a pyramid; who is today's equivalent of the king, archbishop, etc?

Your task 1

Limit the choice to two characters – the king and the peasant. Put them on the pyramid.

Task 7: Medieval buildings

Aim: for pupils to be able to recognise the functions of four different buildings from the Middle Ages

Display photographs of a medieval castle, manor house and cathedral still standing today (see for example pages 83 and 88 of *Contrasts and Connections* and pages 48 and 58 of *Castles and Cathedrals*). Ask pupils why they have survived when all the cottages have disappeared.

Give pupils a selection of pictures of medieval and nineteenth and twentieth-century buildings which they have to sort.

Task 8: Your pathway through Medieval Realms

Aim: for pupils to map out their own objectives for their study of the Middle Ages

(page 1)
This is an information sheet that could also be used at other times as it highlights the three focal points for the unit.

(page 2)
See page 15 for some notes about using this sheet. Pupils fill it in in discussion with the teacher, and could then further decorate it to go in their folder.

It should also be photocopied for your own teacher records.

Use and adapt the sheet however you wish, but we envisage that the theme headings will reflect the three themes outlined on the previous page, and that the numbered lines will list the most important of the tasks you have chosen to tackle.

Section 2: The Battle of Hastings

Aims: (a) to tell the story of the Battle of Hastings; (b) to use the 'bones' of the story to help pupils to understand the main causes of the battle

N.B.1 The Picture Pack includes five pictures from the Bayeux Tapestry and a range of tasks which allow pupils to do detailed work with the Tapestry, including sequencing the main events of the Battle of Hastings.

N.B.2 See also notes on 'The Castle Challenge' (Task 20) which can be used to introduce the whole of Sections 2 and 3 – building on pupils' natural interest in castles – and as a motivating structure for their work in Sections 2 and 3.

Task 9: From across the water...

(*C&C* pp. 68–69)

Aim: for pupils to summarise the events which led to the Battle of Hastings

These information sheets simply set the scene and summarise pages 68–73 of *Contrasts and Connections*.

Task 10: The Battle of Hastings in 1066
(*C&C* pp. 70–73)

Aim: for pupils to be aware of the key people and places involved in the story of the Battle of Hastings

Introduction: Class brainstorms what they already know about the Battle of Hastings. They will probably know the date and the names of the two main protagonists.

Your task:

↔ For question 1 pupils can shade in the sea and land to make reference to the map easier.

↗ Pupils are given an outline map of Europe. They mark on it the place names as found on the original map together with the country of Norway and the place Stamford Bridge. Using the appropriate information on page 73 of *Contrasts*, together with Source 12 on that page, they could write an account of the battle of Stamford Bridge underneath the outline map.

(page 2)
Your task: Question 1 covers the same ground as Task 3 in the Picture Pack but at a higher level in that here pupils have to work out and describe the usefulness of each item themselves.

↗ Question 2: Using all the Bayeux Tapestry pictures they can find (including Picture Sources 1–5 in the Picture Pack and *Contrasts and Connections* pages 68–77) pupils make an extensive list of items which the French soldiers would have taken.

⚒ Pupils then sort the list into items needed for fighting and items needed for living.

Task 11: The story of the Battle of Hastings (*C&C* pp. 74–77)

Aim: for pupils to sequence the events of the Battle of Hastings

✔ There are five pictorial sources from the Bayeux Tapestry in the Picture Pack, together with a simpler sequencing activity.

Your task:

✔ Pupils are given a smaller number of cards with the beginning, middle and end of the story on them. They then do the task as set. When these have been put in chronological order, the teacher introduces the rest of the cards.

✔ Pupils are given a 'comic strip' with some of the pictures and text already stuck down in the correct places. They sort the remainder into chronological order.

✔ For the least able pupils each part of the story could be stuck down, either in pictorial form or in written form so that they only have to match text to picture or vice versa.

✔ Text and pictures could already be matched so that pupils only have to sequence. The number

of cards introduced at any one time will depend on their ability.

↗ Pupils are given only some of the story cards. They try to write their own captions for the pictures which have no text. They compare their versions with other pupils and there could be class discussion as to why the versions might be different.

Task 12: Why was there a 'Battle of Hastings' in 1066? (*C&C* pp. 70–71)

Aim: for pupils to identify causes of the Battle of Hastings

Introduction: Ensure pupils have understood the captions and the story of the Battle of Hastings before moving on to this exercise.

Your task:

✔ Partially complete the table before copying, or in class discussion, leaving pupils only two or three of the most obvious factors to consider.
N.B. The list includes some causes of the Battle of Hastings, some consequences and some factors which are neither.

↗ White out some of the causes in the table before photocopying. Pupils have to complete the table themselves.

(page 2)
Your task: As with the other pieces of extended writing in this material, pupils should use their own paper for this to allow them to put as much or as little text in the gaps as they see fit.

Links: Move pupils on to the 'How did Harold die?' exercise in *Contrasts*, page 77, and do this as a whole class discussion. Some pupils might be able to write up their findings for homework.

After the discussion, pupils could be asked to form their own opinions as to how Harold died. A graph showing which way pupils 'voted' could be produced.

Task 13: The Battle of Hastings: examining the evidence (*C&C* pp. 76–77)

Aim: for pupils to recognise bias in two contrasting sources

↗ You could cut out the numbered sections of the sources and ask pupils to match them to the correct 'bias'.

Task 14: The Battle of Hastings: your own version

Aim: for pupils to see how sources – including biased ones – can be used in their reconstruction of the past

Your task: Don't overstress the role-play aspect of this. The main aim is for pupils to look at the events of the battle – and use the sources, biased or not – to reconstruct the story. To help them focus on the events, we have numbered the main stages of the descriptions in Sources 1 and 2 (in the previous task).

However, once the stories have been written, pupils can compare the different versions and discuss as a class how and why they are different. What problems does this kind of story pose for the historian?

✔ You can add paragraph headings relating to each of the numbered points in Sources 1 and 2 to help pupils construct their story.

✔ Pupils can draw their version of the story.

Task 15: Why did William win the Battle of Hastings? (C&C pp. 76–77)

Aim: for pupils to identify some of the causes of William's victory

This exercise consciously builds on Task 13, revisiting the ideas introduced there.

Your task:

✔ Causes could be cut out so that they can be physically manipulated.

↗ Pupils could go on to compile their own list of, perhaps, three causes, including one 'nonsense' cause, which others have to identify.

Section 3: The Norman Conquest

Task 16: How did William gain control?

(C&C pp. 78–79)

Aim: for pupils to identify three steps William took to gain control of England after the Battle of Hastings

(page 2)

Your task:

↗ Pupils could be asked to predict how William will solve his problems before they receive page 2 of the task.

↔ Pupils can either cut out the problems and solutions and paste them together, or can use the table provided.

✔ Even in this adapted form the language of the three sources is difficult. Read and talk through each source with the pupils beforehand and agree on a clear explanation of what each source means.

✎ Pupils use the 'unadapted' sources on the resource sheet (which equate to Sources 2, 3, 5 and 6 on pages 78–79 of Contrasts) to match with William's problems.

(page 3)

Your task:

✔ You can preselect the burning of Dover Castle and give pupils an outline of a castle (as on page 1 of Task 20). They complete the rest of the drawing themselves.

↔ Pupils should be encouraged to refer to Picture Sources 1–5 from the Bayeux Tapestry to give them ideas for their drawings.

↗ Pupils can use their textbook for ideas about what castles looked like and what ordinary people looked like, or

✔ you can preselect for them pictures which will help them.

Task 17: How did William keep control? (C&C pp. 80–83)

Aim: for pupils to encounter five key features of medieval England which were introduced by William the Conqueror

The subsequent tasks look in detail at the Domesday survey, castles and the feudal system. In this way, these tasks provide some background for pupils' study of life in medieval villages.

Your task:

✔ You could limit the choice to the first two suggestions on page 1 of the task.

↔ You could divide pupils into five groups. Give each group one suggestion. They discuss it amongst themselves and compose arguments to present to the King explaining why theirs is such a good suggestion. Each member of the group is thus an 'expert' concerning that particular suggestion.

The group then presents its arguments to the King (role-played by either the teacher or a member of the class).

Five new groups are then formed combining 'experts' from the previous groups. The groups discuss each suggestion in detail using the expertise from each member. Their aim is to decide on the two **best** suggestions.

↔ The letter to the King can either be completed by the group as a whole or, if they cannot come to an agreement, by individual members of the group.

Task 18: The Domesday Book

(C&C pp. 80–81)

Aims: for pupils to find out the reasons for and the nature of the Domesday survey

This can be used as extension work for any pupils studying Contrasts as Domesday was one subject dealt with in very little detail in the textbook. It also provides useful background to the study of Elton.

Preparation: Enlarge page 3 to A3 size if possible.

Your task:

✔ Photocopy page 3 on to card and cut out each piece of information. Give each pupil one card only.

↗ Having made their list in response to question 1, pupils then write a paragraph explaining in their own words what the King's officials discovered.

(page 4)

Discuss these questions thoroughly before pupils write their answers.

Task 19: Castles (*C&C* pp. 82–83)

Aim: for pupils to use a single picture source to identify some features of William's early castles

N.B. This picture is Source 11 on page 82 of *Contrasts*.

Introduction: We have not used the terminology of motte and bailey. You may wish to introduce it here.

(page 2)
Your task:

✔ Tackle questions 1–4 in class or group discussion. Pupils then answer questions 5–7 on their own.

Task 20: The Castle Challenge

Aim: for pupils to make their own picture of a Norman castle.

The idea of this task is that pupils gradually assemble their own 'cut and paste' picture of a Norman stone castle and then fill it with people.

However, it further aims
i) to reward pupils for hard work and achievement
ii) to provide a motivating structure for pupils' work on the Norman Conquest
iii) to form a basis for pupils' learning about castles and their role in the Norman Conquest of England.

It can be used in a number of different ways. It can be used in its own right to study the importance of castles to William's conquest of Britain (in which case it naturally fits with Task 22).

However, it can also be used as an introduction to and structure for pupils' work on the Battle of Hastings and the Norman Conquest, and can be introduced before Task 9. It is that usage which we will cover first.

Using the Castle Challenge to introduce the Norman Conquest

Most pupils will have seen a castle and be interested in castles generally. This task can use that natural interest to motivate them in their work through Sections 2 and 3 of this material.

Point out that before the Normans came to England there were no castles (although this statement is itself investigated and qualified in SHP's *Castles and Cathedrals*). The building of castles was one of the most obvious changes that William brought to England.

The Castle Challenge is an invitation to the pupils to construct their own picture of a Norman castle over the next (x) weeks. Each time they finish a piece of work on the Battle of Hastings or the Norman Conquest, they will be given another piece of the castle.

It is up to you to decide how the 'rewards' should be assigned. There are six pieces of castle. If you are only tackling two tasks from Sections 2 and 3 you might decide that pupils get three pieces of castle for each piece of work. Or if you are doing six tasks you might want to give them one piece for each finished task.

✔ You could alternatively make a group castle or a class castle towards which everyone's effort contributes. Each time the group/class successfully finishes a task, another component is added to the castle. For such a class castle, the components can be enlarged on card to A3 (or even A2 size in a commercial photocopying shop).

Your task 1: The small inset picture of the whole castle should guide pupils when they are assembling their castle. Each piece has been numbered. It is important that they are given out in numerical order so that they can fit together properly.

✔ For some pupils you may wish to cut the pieces out yourself and help pupils stick them down.

Task 21: Where would you build your castle?

Aim: for pupils to see the reasons why castles were built where they were

Introduction: Pupils could discuss the sites of castles they know.

(page 3)
Your task: Before going on to question 4, check which sites pupils have chosen. If they are obviously poor choices, you should point them in a more suitable direction and discuss reasons before they do any explaining. You could finish with a class vote on the best site.

Task 22: Features of a castle

Aim: for pupils to consider the importance of various features of castles

Your task:

↗ Ask pupils to explain why they have chosen each of the features they have.

↔ Pupils can use a range of sources to provide them with ideas for their writing and drawing.
There are some very detailed reconstruction drawings of castles in SHP's *Castles and Cathedrals*.

↗ The main castle terms could go into pupils' history dictionaries.

Task 23: The feudal system (*C&C* p. 80)

Aim: for pupils to grasp the essential terminology of the feudal system. This forms a valuable background for pupils' study of the medieval village

This is principally intended as a support sheet for users of *Contrasts and Connections*. It personalises the diagram in Source 8 on page 80.

Section 4: Reconstructing medieval villages

Aims
In this section pupils will use different types of evidence to enable them to build up a picture of what

a medieval village might have looked like. They will have opportunities to work with

- photographic evidence
- archaeologists' plans
- artists' reconstructions
- a story.

The Picture Pack also contains twelve illustrations of different aspects of life in a medieval village which can be used as a prelude to the following activities.

We use the structure of *Contrasts* – studying the village of Wharram Percy first (where the evidence is archaeological), followed by the village of Elton (where the evidence is mainly documentary).

Task 24: The lost village of Wharram Percy in Yorkshire (*C&C* pp. 84–85)

Aim: for pupils to use some archaeological evidence and to see its value for a historian

(page 1)
Introduction: This is an information page and should ideally be used for class discussion:

Compare the two homes. How are they different and how are they similar?

What sort of people would live in the cottage?

What sort of people would live in the house?

Pupils can add further labels to their copies of the drawings.

Which parts of the buildings would decay first and why?

(page 2)
The aerial photograph can also be found on page 84 of *Contrasts and Connections*.

Your task:
✔ For questions 4 and 5 you can tell the pupils what the lines and shapes are. They then transfer this information to the archaeologist's report.

(page 4)
↗ Follow this up with discussion as to the difficulties of building up a picture of medieval life when there are no 'built' remains and only fragments to examine – thus leading into the Alice story which follows, which allows imaginative reconstruction to take over where the evidence tails off.

Task 25: Alice's Unhappy Day

Aim: for pupils to become interested in Wharram Percy and the people who might have lived in the village

This story is an imaginative reconstruction by the author of life in Wharram Percy. The story is set in the 1330s. Alice is 12 years old. She will re-appear as a young woman in a later story (see Task 38) when the Black Death comes to the village of Wharram Percy in 1348.

The purpose of the story is initially to raise pupils'

interest in the village through their interest in Alice. The ideal way to use it is therefore to tell or read the story to the class; to discuss it using any of the ideas below and then go on to whichever of Tasks 26–29 you intend to use, or indeed to go straight into Section 5 which focuses on life in a medieval village.

↔ Teacher reads the story. Pupils re-tell parts of it. For other ways of telling or reading the story, see detailed notes on the other Alice story (Task 38).

↔ Pupils read the story. They look at our three illustrations for the story. They then choose one other moment in the story and draw a picture to illustrate it.

↔ Class discussion. What is the most likely reason why baby Walter died?

↗ Individual research into herbal cures, lotions, potions, etc.

Task 26: The buildings of Wharram Percy

Aim: for pupils to become familiar with six of the important buildings to be found in a medieval village

Preparation: For this task teachers and pupils have the choice of using the full-colour reconstruction drawing of Wharram Percy (page 85 of *Contrasts*) or the black and white outline of it on page 3 of the task.

Your task:
↔ Pupils can draw buildings in the boxes, rather than 'cutting and pasting'.

↗ Discuss what type of house the priest might have lived in. (Look back at page 1 to help.) Pupils make an extra box and draw in the appropriate type of house.

↗ Pupils look at the artist's reconstruction and draw in the mud tracks and pathways on their archaeological plan.

Task 27: The archaeology game

Aim: for pupils to practise some of the basic disciplines of the archaeologist

Your task:
↔ Pupils complete the fragments to make a 'whole' jug and shoe.

↔ Pupils 'test' each other by drawing in more 'medieval objects' and asking their partners which grid references they are in.

↔ Class discussion: What were these objects used for? Who might have used them? These are important questions to ask about all objects.

(page 2)
Your task: Teacher needs to lead the session by going through the activity with one or two of the objects to ensure that the pupils know what they are doing.

✔ Pupils are only given one strip of the 'grid'. They colour in the objects that come from modern times.

☑ Pupils write the names of the medieval objects under the correct picture.

(page 3)

Your task:

↔ Go through this activity with the whole group. Discussion re question 'Who might have used it?' Pupils should recognise that it is quite difficult to answer this question because several types of people could have used the object. They need more evidence. Encourage them to 'best guess'.

↗ Pupils work out possible former occupants of this medieval cottage.

↔ Pupils draw the person actually using or wearing one of the objects.

↗ Introduce anachronism. Pupils draw a medieval person using one of the modern objects.

Task 28: How can we reconstruct the village of Elton? (*C&C* pp. 86–87)

Aim: for pupils to see the use of documentary evidence in reconstructing the past

If you tackled the Domesday enquiry, pupils will already have been introduced to the existence of written evidence about Elton.

Your task:

☑ You could pre-select two or three categories from which pupils have to choose.

Task 29: The buildings of Elton

(*C&C* pp. 88–89)

Aim: for pupils to use some pictorial and written sources to develop their own ideas about what the village of Elton might have looked like

As we have stressed in the TRB for *Contrasts and Connections*, in trying to reconstruct the village of Elton there are no right answers. There are wrong ones – in that they might conflict with the little available evidence – but it is a good opportunity to encourage pupils to risk their own ideas about the past when even the experts have no clear idea of what Elton might have been like.

Your task:

↗ You could tell pupils that all the sources except two are records of village repairs or building work. What kind of sources are the other two?

☑ Teacher cuts sources into strips and pupils have only one 'strip' of sources to do.

☑ Teacher completes the names of the buildings him/herself. Separate the sources from the answers. Pupils match the sets together.

(page 3)

Your task:

↔ Pupils place appropriate sources on top of, or next to the picture sources on pages 86–89 of *Contrasts and Connections*.

↗ Pupils could be given page references for pictures in a range of reference books which show what each of these buildings looked like. They match the sources to the pictures.

↗ After completing the table pupils can go directly on to questions 2 and 3 on page 89 of *Contrasts and Connnections*.

Section 5: Living and working in a medieval village

Aims

This section is at the heart of the unit. It aims to explore various aspects of medieval life. The worksheets here are inseparable from the work provided in the Picture Pack – which uses the large-size visuals to heighten pupils' interest in the period and as a stimulus for their their own questions about it.

Using the Picture Pack pupils can work in groups of three or four to examine one pictorial source very carefully and should be encouraged to think of any question at all, however simple, to ask about their particular picture. (See Picture Pack Teachers' Notes page 5.)

This can be done
a) as a whole class activity, with the teacher giving substantial help; or
b) by the group using available textbooks, the process of deduction, their own knowledge, informed 'guesses', and asking people from other groups to help them.

Task 30: Inside a peasant's cottage

(*C&C* p. 98)

Aim: for pupils to build up their own mental picture of the inside of a peasant's house

Introduction: The picture is in fact a reconstruction drawing by an archaeologist of what the inside of a Wharram Percy cottage would have looked like. It also appears in *Contrasts and Connections*, page 98. This drawing is the model for the description of Alice's cottage in Task 25. The story in Task 25 could therefore be used as the general introduction to this section and to lead into this task in particular.

Task 31: What jobs did people do in the Middle Ages? (*C&C* pp. 90–91)

Aim: for pupils to use pictorial source material to identify some jobs which people did in the Middle Ages

This exercise is based entirely on pictures in the Picture Pack.

Your task: It is not intended that you give out all three pages of the table together. It would be too daunting for most pupils.

☑ Pupils could work in groups, taking one page for a whole group, or one source for a whole group, with other groups taking other pages.

☑ The teacher could have flashcards with the missing answers. Pupils match the cards to the blanks.

↗ The words from the resource sheet can be introduced (or re-introduced) and added to pupils' history dictionaries.

↗ The teacher could white out some of the information in the table.

🔨 Pupils could be given selected picture sources and the column headings for the table, and asked to create and complete a table on their own.

Task 32: The peasants' year (C&C pp. 92–93)

Aim: for pupils to identify some tasks a peasant farmer would have to undertake

Your task: This task builds on Task 31. You can give pupils either the full Picture Pack to look at, or
☑ pre-select only half a dozen images from it.

(page 2)
Your task:
☑ You could select only certain months for pupils to work on.

☑ Some of the prompt lines are suggested by the 'All year round' paragraph from the chart. Make sure pupils are guided towards this for the months of April, May and December.

Task 33: How did people dress in the Middle Ages?

Aim: for pupils to compare the way people dressed in the Middle Ages with the way people dress to do similar jobs today

☑ Pupils could work in pairs. One person takes the source showing a man, the other takes the source showing a woman.

Task 34: What did people eat in the Middle Ages? (C&C pp. 99–101)

Aim: for pupils to compare the food eaten by the rich and poor

Links: This links into the enquiry 'The poor and the rich at home' on pages 98–101 of Contrasts and Connections.

Your task: One aim here is to allow pupils to develop their skills of source selection. However, if you wish:
☑ You can pre-select certain pictures from the Picture Pack to match the learning needs of the pupils.

☑ Pupils complete the table by drawing the item of food from the pictorial source in the second column.

☑ Pupils work in pairs. The more able writer completes the third column after discussion with his or her partner.

(page 2)
Your task: These sources can be found on pages 88,

99,100, and 101 of Contrasts and Connections.
☑ The four written sources vary greatly in difficulty. You could allow pupils to choose one source only to interrogate.

↔ Check that pupils understand the written sources before doing this activity.

(pages 4 and 5)
Both tasks refer back to the tables pupils have just completed. Suggest they draw some meat, dairy produce, drink and bread to start them off. You could give out copies of the resource sheet to help pupils with their drawings – but emphasise that their drawings do not need to be perfect renderings of each item of food.

Task 35: Not a medieval village

Aim: for pupils to use their knowledge of medieval village life to spot anachronisms

Your task:
↗ You could develop this further by asking pupils to indicate how they know a feature is anachronistic.

Section 6: The 'Black Death'

Aims
We have used the Black Death as a lens through which to look at medieval village life. The aim is for pupils to see the impact this disease would have had upon individuals. We have therefore returned to a character we have already introduced (Alice from Wharram Percy) to personalise the tragedy of the Black Death.

We deal in detail with the causes and course of the Black Death. The links with incurable and deadly diseases such as AIDS are obvious and should provide teachers with opportunities to compare contemporary attitudes and experiences with those of the Middle Ages.

Finally, the tasks in this section aim to use a wider range of source material than previous sections – and to encourage pupils to see the usefulness of each type of source.

Task 36: What was the 'Black Death' and what caused it? (C&C pp. 124–25)

Aim: for pupils to grasp the chronology of the Black Death, and the causes of the disease

For the preliminary information sheet we have simplified the explanation of the Black Death to that of bubonic plague only, although in Task 39 we have gone into the distinction between bubonic and pneumonic plague which forms the basis for the first section of work on page 124 of Contrasts and Connections.

(page 2)
Your task:
☑ For question 1 you could underline the place names in the timeline before making photocopies.

☑ For question 5 you could give pupils date headings for each new paragraph when they write their account.

↔ As an alternative to question 5: rather than write an account of the spread of the plague, pupils could draw a comic strip version of what happened.

↔ A further alternative: pupils could imagine they are a stowaway on one of the ships which has plague. They describe how they escape from the ship when everyone else is in quarantine.

(page 3)

↗ Pupils could alternatively use the descriptions in Source 4 on page 125 of *Contrasts and Connections*.

(page 5)

Your task: This can be used as a basis for class discussion. Transfer the diagram to an OHP acetate and fill it in together.

Discussion as to the link between dirt and disease and why medieval people did not make the link. Stress that people had not discovered the existence of germs in the fourteenth century.

Use the text on page 124 of *Contrasts and Connections* to help in completing the diagram.

Task 37: Examining the evidence about the Black Death (*C&C* pp. 124–25)

Aim: for pupils to interrogate two sources about the Black Death

Your task:
This task should be done in groups or class discussion.

☑ Pupils could do only the first two questions – i.e. page 1 of the task.

Task 38: Alice's Wedding Day

Aim: for pupils to understand and empathise with the situation of people in Wharram Percy facing the onset of the Black Death

Introduction: Remind pupils what they have already found out about Alice from the earlier story (Task 25). Encourage them to remember as much as they can about her.
N.B. The wedding is arranged for 15 August, a religious holiday (the Assumption of the Virgin), which explains why the villagers are not at work!

Telling the story
You can read the story to the pupils. This is followed by one of:

a) ☑ Class discussion as they try to remember all the things that happened to Alice and Stephen. The teacher helps by noting things down on the board.

b) ✎ Pupils are given the illustrations for the story to sequence.

c) ☑ Pupils are given the story as shown except that the captions are whited out and they have to write their own captions to the pictures after hearing the story read.

d) ↗ Pupils write their own version of the story.

Task 39: Bubonic or pneumonic plague? (*C&C* p. 124)

Aim: for pupils to realise that two different diseases are thought to have contributed to the Black Death

Task 40: The Black Death in Wharram Percy

Aim: for pupils to reach their own conclusions about the effects of the Black Death on individuals in Wharram Percy

Your task: You might prefer to do this through class discussion, with the class findings recorded on the board.

Task 41: Sources about the Black Death

Aim: for pupils to reflect on the different types of source material they have used to investigate the Black Death and to assess the usefulness of each type

Your task:

☑ Pupils are given only one or two sources to analyse.

☑ Each source is analysed by a small group of pupils. They present their findings to the rest of the class. Only after each group has presented its findings are decisions made as to the usefulness or otherwise of the sources.

Section 7: Towns, travel and trade

Aims
The main aim of this section is to highlight some of the differences between town and village life.

This section is not so crucial a part of the 'core' of the unit as the sections on the medieval villages, but it is interesting in its own right, and introduces a level of complexity to the picture of medieval life which may well be accessible to most pupils.

Task 42: The growth of Ludlow
(*C&C* pp. 108–109)

Aim: for pupils to identify key features of medieval Ludlow

Ludlow was a planned Norman 'new town'. There were twenty or more such towns in England.

Preparation: Ideally blow up pages 2 and 3 to A3 size

Your task:

☑ Pupils are given fewer descriptions to digest!

↗ Pupils choose two written sources and try to draw reconstructions of what they are describing.

↗ Pupils read the sources on page 108 of *Contrasts* and use information from those to help them match the sources to the parts of the map they describe.

Task 43: Trouble in Mill Street

Aim: for pupils to recognise the important role of traders and craftsmen in town life

This story is an imaginative reconstruction of life in Ludlow in the Middle Ages. It is based on a true story, but a story which actually took place in London. We have transferred the events to Ludlow in the thirteenth or fourteenth century when the town was a strong local and regional trading centre.

Pupils can have the story read to them or can read it themselves. For general ideas about introducing the story, see the notes on the Alice story (Task 25).

↔ Tell the story to the class. Follow up with a class discussion trying to remember all the things that happened to James and Growler. The teacher helps by noting things down on the board.

✔ The teacher prepares some flashcards with the main points of the story on them. Pupils are asked to sequence these cards and then to illustrate them.

↗ Discuss why James's parents were so frightened of the pillory.

Links:

↗ Pupils do some research of their own into medieval punishments. What was used for which crimes? Which punishments were considered most severe? This is gone into in some detail in the enquiry 'Could you get justice in the Middle Ages?' on pages 120–123 of *Contrasts and Connections*.

Task 44: Shops and traders in Ludlow

(*C&C* pp. 110–11)

Aim: for pupils to identify some of the trades represented in medieval Ludlow

Your task:

↔ Discuss question 1 in class before pupils write their answers. They might have ideas for more than one shop or business in each street, e.g. Mill Street might include both a mill and a baker's.

↔ For question 2 pupils make the list of clues and also colour or mark with a cross the clues on the picture itself. The shoemaker's shop can be found in colour on page 110 of *Contrasts*.

↗ For question 4, pupils could use Source 12 on page 111 of *Contrasts* (which is found as Picture Source 18 in the Picture Pack) to help them draw a complete shop front rather than just a shop sign.

↗ Pupils use all the evidence on pages 108–11 of *Contrasts* to draw up a complete list of trades

which went on in Ludlow. Working in groups they design and make a collage/wall display of Ludlow on market day with each stall representing a trade or occupation.

↗ Pupils use evidence from other books, pictures and medieval maps of other towns to make a list of **other** trades and occupations which might have gone on in medieval towns.

Task 45: Did people travel much in the Middle Ages? (*C&C* pp. 106–107)

Aim: for pupils to compare means of transport in the Middle Ages with means of transport today

This sets the scene for the board game which forms the main exercise on this subject.

↔ Pupils could be given a copy of the resource sheet, which includes outlines of Sources 18, 23 and 24 on pages 106–107 of *Contrasts*, to help them with ideas for how people travelled.

↗ Pupils could go on to make a list of all the different people who did have to travel in the Middle Ages, using *Contrasts* Sources 19–25 on pages 106–107.

Task 46: The Race to the King's Court

Aim: for pupils to identify what problems travellers faced in the Middle Ages

In this board game the pupils are musicians travelling to the King's court during the Middle Ages. The first to arrive is going to become rich and famous because the King is a great lover of music and will pay a lot for a good musician.

There are some obstacles and setbacks on the way (bad news) but some people or things also help the travellers (good news). The challenges they meet on the way are simplified versions of the source material on pages 104–107 of *Contrasts*.

Preparation: The game board should preferably be blown up to A3 size.

You could make two copies of each of the good and bad news sheets. Preferably photocopy bad news on to one colour card and good news on to another colour.

Your task 1: Pupils can play the game for themselves – it will introduce them to the main troubles involved in travelling in the Middle Ages.

Your task 2: This both extends the activity upwards, and also makes a strong link with *Contrasts and Connections*. If you are not using *Contrasts*, or if you do not want to use this extension activity, white out or cover this second activity before photocopying.

✔ After the game or as a prelude to it pupils can be given the bad news and good news cards cut in half and they have to match the captions and the pictures.

↗ Pupils could write an account of their journey as a follow-up to the game.

Section 8: How religious were people in the Middle Ages?

Aims

This section is intended to show pupils just how important religion was in the everyday life of people during the Middle Ages. It is important for teachers to draw out the comparison between today's attitudes to religion and those which were prevalent 900 years ago.

Task 47: Heaven and hell (C&C pp. 112–13)

Introduction: Pupils read text and discuss it with the teacher. How are attitudes different today? How many pupils still go to church? How many pupils believe in God? From where do pupils nowadays get most of their ideas about religion?

Preparation: Photocopy the outline picture of the wall painting for each pupil.

(page 2)

Your task: This task mirrors closely the questions in *Contrasts*, page 113.

↔ Pupils should discuss their ideas for question 9 before attempting to write their answers.

✔ Pupils could be given only a quarter section of the picture with the appropriate questions.

Your task 2:

✔ Pupils could be given a smaller number of views to consider.

↗ Pupils cut out the medieval pictures and speech bubbles and stick them on to a piece of A4 paper. They write an explanation underneath as to why people would have thought like this in the Middle Ages.

Task 48: Who would go to heaven?

(*C&C* pp. 112–13)

Aim: for pupils to examine three sources from the Middle Ages which tell us about medieval beliefs

This is extension work for those pupils who have completed Task 47.

The sources are simplified versions of those found on pages 113–14 of *Contrasts*. Pupils could answer the questions on page 113 in class discussion after they have completed the tasks.

Your task:

↔ Pupils underline the key words and phrases in each source before they give their written explanation.

✔ Pupils discuss these questions rather than write their answers down.

(page 2)

Your task: Pupils should look at the imagery in the original painting to help them draw their pictures of heaven and hell, but they should show the fate of the three people described in Sources 1–3.

You could copy the finished murals on to OHP

acetate, project them on to the wall and photograph the resulting 'mural' for the pupils' work file.

Task 49: The Game of Heaven and Hell

Aim: for pupils to gain insight into what medieval people believed about heaven and hell

This board game is based on snakes and ladders. Pupils are travelling through life. As they progress they find that certain things they do are more likely to get them to heaven than others. The aim of course is to get to heaven. The learning aim, however, is to appreciate what actions medieval people thought would earn them a place in heaven.

The game also introduces the important concept of 'purgatory' which has been omitted from the previous tasks.

Preparation: Photocopy the game board to as large as possible a size.

Photocopy the angels and devils on to different-coloured card. N.B. If you are really pressed for time, the game can be played without the angel and devil cards as long as pupils keep an accurate record of their fates on their score sheet.

Your task: Pupils will need to keep a tally of what happens to them in the game. Each time they land on a devil's tail or an angel's ladder, they write down the action, and note what reward it receives.

N.B.1 You may need to introduce some words before playing the game (friar, relic, fast, pilgrimage, Lent).

N.B.2 The final square of the game is not death or heaven or hell, so if they do reach the end they should go back to square one and continue on life's way.

At the end of the game, before pupils record their fate (question 4), they can discuss who they think has been the most wicked and the most virtuous.

↗ Class discussion as to what crimes/good deeds would merit these fates nowadays.

Section 9: King Henry and the Church

Aims

This section returns to the core entitlement for **Medieval Realms**, and should be on everyone's pathway. The aim is to highlight how important it was for a medieval king to control the Church.

Task 50: The murder of an archbishop

(*C&C* pp. 130–131)

Aim: for pupils to practise their sequencing skills, as in Task 11, and to summarise the story of the murder of Becket

Introduction: If the previous tasks on religion have been undertaken then they will form a solid foundation for these exercises. If not, then some initial summary will be needed to demonstrate the power and importance of the Church. For this purpose you could use just the first page of Task 47. Most importantly pupils must be aware of the role of the priest as it will highlight the importance that a king would attach to controlling the priests if he was to control the country.

Pupils may need to recap some of the key vocabulary from the earlier sections on the Norman Conquest.

Your task:

☑ Only use three pictures and three explanations.

☑ Have parts of the explanations already pasted under the pictures. Pupils fill in the missing bits.

☑ Pupils paste the information on to a timeline which already has the dates put in the correct order.

Task 51: King Henry's reign

Aim: for pupils to practise their timeline skills, and to reinforce the sequence of the events themselves

Your task: This is an extension exercise – to reinforce in pupils' minds the fact that a vertical timeline (as used in many books they will come across) has the same basic function as a horizontal timeline.

Task 52: The death of Thomas Becket

(*C&C* pp 132–33)

Aim: for pupils to see how written and visual sources can be cross-referenced to one another

This task revisits the concept of bias.

Task 53: The Murder of Thomas Becket: a play

Aim: for pupils to read the story of the conflict between Thomas and Henry, and to find out more about the roles of the King and the Archbishop, and the conflict between king and Church.

Preparation: If you feel that this play is too long, you may wish to split it up into smaller sections – giving small groups part of the story to work on.

The narrator's role is very important in holding the play together, and giving directions in his/her text. Teachers could play this role themselves.

There is obviously no need to learn the lines.

The play also highlights some of the symbolic objects associated with king and archbishop – the crown, the mitre etc. – and uses these to dramatise the conflict between the two parties. The impact of the play will be increased if you make a few of these objects for use in the play. Card, glue, felt-tip pens, sugar paper, silver foil, etc. should suffice.

There are no female parts in the play, which underlines how male-oriented much medieval political history tends to be. However, girls can of course play male roles.

Using the play: This play can be used to introduce the subject of Henry and Becket. In this case stop the action at 'Henry had a plan' (on page 3) and discuss with the class what they expect to happen next – what is Henry's plan going to be?

Do the same after 'Then King Henry roared...' on page 4. What will happen next?

⟷ After reading the play, find pictures in reference books showing a king or archbishop with the symbolic objects mentioned in it.

⟷ Discuss to what extent Henry was to blame for the argument and to what extent Becket was to blame.

Section 10: King John and the barons

Aims

In this section we turn to a second kind of problem facing the medieval king – the relationship with the barons.

This section is probably less central to the core entitlement for the unit – but it can be used to support and extend the work in *Contrasts and Connections*, pages 134–37.

While the aim is to look at how John clashed with his barons, as a way into this we look in some detail at King John, his reputation, and his actions while he was king.

Task 54: King John – an evil king?

(*C&C* pp. 134–35)

Aim: for pupils to compare two images of John – through comparing a picture source with a written source

Your task:

☑ For question 1 you can provide pupils with the missing words which they then use to complete the sentences.

⟷ Pupils colour in the four aspects of the picture that make John look good (i.e. most of the picture!) They label each feature appropriately. the Latin words.

(page 3)

Your task:

↗ Pupils are only given the source. They have to find five unpleasant things that the monk said about King John.

⟷ Pupils underline those parts of the source that match the list of things that the monk said about King John.

↗ Pupils are pointed to Sources 1–5 on page 134 of *Contrasts* to find further accusations against John.

⟷ Pupils complete the amended drawing of King John **after** a discussion with the teacher about bias, propaganda etc.

✔ Suggestions are given to the pupils about how they might adapt this picture, e.g. should the king be standing or sitting, should he have a weapon in his hand?

↔ Each subsequent pictorial interpretation by the pupils is discussed and the new pictures are graded according to 'awfulness'!

Discuss how people from long ago saw John in different ways, just as they now see him in varying degrees of 'awfulness'.

Task 55: What did John do when he was King? (C&C pp. 134–35)

Aims: for pupils to investigate some of John's failures and successes as a king

Your task: These actions of John may need substantial classroom discussion for them to have any meaning – particularly the more generalised ones. There is a fuller explanation of the background to John's reign – and a summary of the problems he inherited from his brother Richard – on page 136 of *Contrasts*.

✔ Pupils could be given fewer cards.

Task 56: Magna Carta – the Great Charter? (C&C pp. 136–37)

Aim: for pupils to identify the main features of Magna Carta

Introduction: Begin the lesson by asking pupils about their own wants and needs. Pupils construct a list, either orally or on paper, of demands they would like to make of their Mum or Dad (depending on who is in charge at home!)

After this is done, the teacher asks which pupils have included any likely demands that the siblings might make in the list, i.e. how selfish is each list of demands?

Through discussion, make links with the demands of the Magna Carta.

Pupils can then write their own explanation of what the Magna Carta was.

(resource sheet)
This page is intended for teacher-led, whole-class discussion.

Alternatively pupils can work in small groups. Each group is given a block of questions from the resource sheet. They discuss these questions amongst themselves. One person records the results of their discussion and reports their findings to the rest of the class.

↗ Pupils can then go on to tackle questions 4, 5 and 6 on page 137 of *Contrasts*.

Section 11: King Richard and the Peasants' Revolt

Aims
The third problem facing medieval kings which we look at is the problem of the peasants. Pupils should be well aware of the role of the peasant in medieval society by now and the lives peasants led.

The aim is to focus on the events of the revolt rather than its causes.

Task 57: The Peasants' Revolt
(C&C pp. 140–43)

Aim: for pupils to be able to sequence the events of the Peasants' Revolt

Links: As explained above, in these support materials we have focused on the events of the revolt rather than the causes, as they are complex. The corresponding material in *Contrasts* is on page 140 (the long written source 1) and page 142 (the two versions of the events at Smithfield).

However, if you want to investigate the causes yourself or if you need more background to the revolt, there is a summary on page 141 of *Contrasts*.

Introduction: Remind pupils about their work on Magna Carta. Try to recall which group of people was *not* represented in the demands which were made. Recall also that *most people in England were peasants*.

Discuss how people can try to make sure their demands are met. What methods do people use when they have no money, no power and no influence?

Finally, locate the event on the large timeline of the Middle Ages. Point out that the revolt happened *after* the Black Death. Discuss how this event might have affected the peasants.

In these materials we have not gone into the links between the Black Death and the Peasants' Revolt, but in summary: as a result of the Black Death the supply of labour had gone down, so that wages had generally gone up. As a result of this the lords were enforcing feudal dues more rigidly than before and trying to tax the peasants' income more harshly.

Your task: There are various ways of introducing the story (which is a greatly simplified and abbreviated version of Source 1 on page 140 of *Contrasts*).

↔ You can tell it yourself.

↗ You could read and discuss the long version in *Contrasts*.

↙ You could cut the cards in half and ask pupils to match the captions and pictures.

↗ You could cut out the six story cards and ask pupils to sequence them.

↗ Pupils can read the story in *Contrasts*, then you can give them page 2 but with some of the text boxes blanked out. Pupils have to add the missing text.

You can give pupils page 2 with all the text blanked out, i.e. they have only the pictorial part of the comic strip. They read the story in *Contrasts* and write the story in the boxes underneath each picture.

 Pupils can re-write the story in their own words without the help of the pictures.

N.B. The two empty boxes at the foot of page 2 will be used for the task on page 6.

 For question 2 you can complete some of the boxes on the map before copying.

(page 4)
Your task:

Class discuss what they think might be going to happen when the King meets the peasants. Note their ideas on the board.

Task 30 from the Picture Pack can be used instead of pages 4–6 of this task.

Discussion points:

To follow up this discussion pupils could draw a picture of King Richard either as his loyal supporters or as his enemies (to revisit the ideas in the King John activity in Task 54).

They can then choose words from the text on page 5 to write underneath their drawing.

(page 6)
Your task:

Pupils can write their sentences in the style of the other six boxes.

Section 12: Conclusions

Aims
These last two tasks return to some of the ideas introduced at the start of the unit.

Task 58: Important events of the Middle Ages

Aim: for pupils to practise their timeline skills, strengthen their sense of the chronology of the Middle Ages, and to recap some of the main events

Your task: Pupils might add the Battle of Hastings, the Black Death, and the murder of Thomas Becket.

Task 59: What were the Middle Ages really like?

Aim: for pupils to update their judgement about the period

Introduction: Refer pupils back to Task 5.

Your task:

Pupils could add other adjectives they think describe the Middle Ages.

They could make a 'collage' of drawings and pictures to surround each word.

1

You will need

- pen or pencil

```
◆ HISTORY DICTIONARY

The important words          My explanation of them

history
        _____

        _____
```

What is history?

History is about the **past.** History is about **what happened** in the past. History is about **people** in the past and **what they did and thought and felt**. **You** are one of those people. What you did in the past is history.

   Historians write down what they think are the **important things about the past.** These are examples of some important events in my past:

■ I was born in 1954
■ When I was four I had to go into hospital to have my tonsils out
■ In 1965 I moved to a new school.

Your task

Make your own list of important events in your past.

Some important events in my past are:

_____

_____

_____

_____

_____

_____

_____

_____

2

You will need
- pen or pencil
- scissors
- glue

♦ HISTORY DICTIONARY

The important words	My explanation of them
chronological order	_____
	_____
	_____
timeline	_____
	_____
	_____

Putting events into chronological order

Historians write about the events of the past which they think are important. They usually write them down in the order in which they happened – **chronological order**.

Sometimes they show this by putting the events on a **timeline**. They put the things which happened first at the beginning. They put the things which happened last at the end.

This is what part of my timeline would look like:

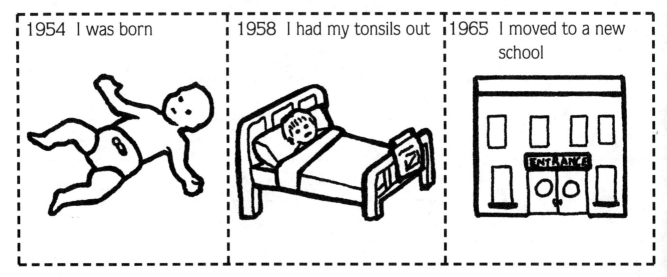

1954 I was born

1958 I had my tonsils out

1965 I moved to a new school

Your task

On the next page is a blank timeline. Record the important events of your past on it. Try to find something important for every year of your life. Don't worry if you can't remember the exact dates, just try to put things in the right chronological order.

1. Start in the first square with the year you were born.
2. At the top of each square write in something important for that year of your life.
3. Draw a picture of each of these important events.

19......

19......

19......

19......

19......

19......

3

You will need
- pen or pencil
- scissors

◆ **HISTORY DICTIONARY**

The important words   **My explanation of them**

The Middle Ages

_____

_____

Putting periods of history into chronological order

Historians organise the past into periods of time. They give each of these periods a name. In this unit you will be studying the period of time called **the Middle Ages**. Let's see whereabouts in history this period fits.

On the next two sheets there are two sets of cards. On page 2 there is a set of period cards. On page 3 there is a set of description cards.

Your task

1. Cut out the cards on both pages.
2. Match up each period card with a description card. For example:

Tudor and Stuart times, AD1485–1714

Elizabeth Tudor

Kings and queens with the surname Tudor or Stuart ruled over England

3. When you have matched all the cards correctly, set the pairs out in chronological order as a timeline. Your timeline should begin and end like this:

Roman times, 43 BC–AD 410

People who came from Rome ruled over England

Modern times, AD 1945 onwards

The age of space travel and computers

☞

Period cards

Cut out these cards and match each one with a description card.

Roman times, 43 BC–AD 410	Tudor and Stuart times, AD 1485–1714	First part of the twentieth century, AD 1901–39
Saxon and Viking times, AD 410–1066	Georgian times, AD 1714–1837	The Second World War, AD 1939–45
The Middle Ages, AD 1066–1485	Victorian times, AD 1837–1901	Modern times, AD 1945 onwards

👉

Description cards

Cut out these cards and match each one with a period card.

✂

Nearly every country in the world was affected by this six-year war

A long period between the time of the Vikings and the beginning of the Tudor period

The First World War happened during this time

Saxons from Germany, and later Viking invaders from Denmark, settled in England

The age of space travel and computers

People who came from Rome ruled over England

Elizabeth Tudor

Kings and queens with the surname Tudor or Stuart ruled over England

Queen Victoria was Queen of England

Most rulers were called George!

4

You will need
• pen or pencil

♦ **HISTORY DICTIONARY**

The important words	My explanation of them
historical source	_____
	_____

How we find out about the past: historical sources

When I had grown up it was hard to remember all the things I had done. So I asked my mum to help me.

Mum was a good **historical source**. She was very good at helping me to find out about the past.

Mum was a good historical source

Mum remembered me having my tonsils out. She had kept my hospital record card. This was another very good historical source.

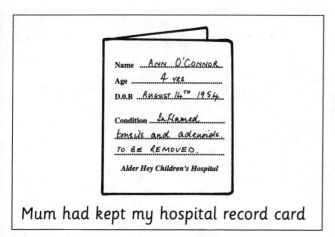

Name ...Ann..O'Connor...
Age ....4 yrs........
D.O.B ..August 14th 1954..
Condition ...Inflamed...
tonsils and adenoids.
TO BE REMOVED.
Alder Hey Children's Hospital

Mum had kept my hospital record card

Mum had kept a photograph of me when I came out of hospital. I liked this historical source. I liked it because it showed me what I looked like when I was little.

My photograph of when I was little

I asked Mum if she had kept my tonsils in a bottle. She said 'No!' I wish she had. That would have been a great historical source!

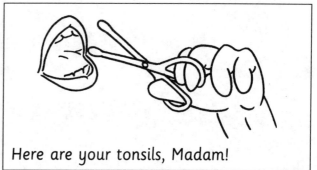

Here are your tonsils, Madam!

4

☞

●○○

Historians can use all sorts of sources. For example, the historical sources which I used to find out about having my tonsils out were:
- ■ my mum
- ■ my hospital record card
- ■ a photograph of myself
- ■ my own memories.

What historical sources did you use to help you to remember important events in your past? Perhaps you had an old photograph of yourself? Perhaps you had kept some of your old toys?

Your task ✎

Make a list or draw pictures of some of the historical sources you have got at home which could be used as evidence about you. Your teacher will be able to help you. You could also ask someone at home to help you.

The sources which I could use as evidence about myself are

_____   _____   _____

_____   _____   _____

_____   _____   _____

MEDIEVAL REALMS SUPPORT MATERIALS

5

You will need
- pen or pencil

♦ **HISTORY DICTIONARY**

The important words	My explanation of them
evidence	_____
	_____

Using historical sources to find out about the Middle Ages

Historians use many different historical sources, such as photographs and drawings, buildings, the clothes people wore, or the things people wrote.

They can all give us important information about the past. Historians collect all these sources together. When they have collected them together they use them as **evidence** about the past.

On the next two pages are two historical sources about the Middle Ages. There is evidence in these sources about life at that time and about the things that people did. You can also find both these pictures in your Picture Pack as Picture Sources 20 and 4.

Your task

1. Look at the picture on page 2. Some of the things the people in the picture are doing have been given a letter. In the table below we have listed these activities. Match each letter to a description.

description	letter
■ sawing a plank of wood ■ giving orders to workers ■ drilling a hole in some wood ■ putting tiles on a roof ■ climbing up a ladder	

2. Look at the picture on page 3. Describe what is happening.

_____

_____

_____

3. These two pictures give us different impressions of the Middle Ages. Underline in blue pen the words which describe what is going on in the picture on page 2. Underline in red pen the words which describe what is going on in the picture on page 3.

peaceful   clever

dangerous   beautiful

cruel   violent

hardworking

Fighting

☞

Your task
Look at all the sources on pages 64–65 of *Contrasts and Connections*. Choose one word from the list on the first page of this task to describe what is happening in each source. The first one has been done for you. (You can use the same word about two or more sources.)

Source 1 *cruel* _____   Source 6 _____

Source 2 _____   Source 7 _____

Source 3 _____   Source 8 _____

Source 4 _____   Source 9 _____

Source 5 _____   Source 10 _____

 Historians disagree about what the Middle Ages were really like. As you discover more evidence about the Middle Ages you will be able to make up your own mind.

- You will examine more pictures
- You will hear stories
- You will read written evidence
- You might visit medieval buildings
- You will read legal papers
- You might visit a museum.

Will you think they were violent and cruel times? **or**

Will you think they were peaceful and hardworking times? **or**

Will you think they were a mixture of both?

At the end of the course you will be able to discuss these questions with the rest of the class.

You will need
- pen or pencil
- scissors
- glue

♦ HISTORY DICTIONARY

The important words	My explanation of them
peasant	_____
archbishop	_____
nun	_____
baron	_____

What kind of people lived in the Middle Ages?

On the next two pages there are pictures of five men and three women who lived in the Middle Ages.

■ One was a king
■ Two were rich
■ Three were poor
■ Two worked for the Church.

Your task

1. Cut out each figure.
2. Glue the king on to one piece of paper.
3. Glue the two rich people on to another piece of paper.
4. Glue the three poor people on to another piece of paper.
5. Glue the two people who belong to the Church on to a fourth piece of paper.
6. Parts of their clothing or their equipment are missing. All the missing items are on page 4. Find the missing items for each person, cut them out and glue them underneath each figure, like this:

Wat Tyler. He led the peasants in their fight against the King in 1381

gloves

sickle

hood

6

Medieval people

King William the Conqueror. He beat King Harold at the Battle of Hastings in 1066

A nun sewing the Bayeux Tapestry in 1077

Wat Tyler. He led the peasants in their fight against the King in 1381

A peasant woman trying to keep her family clean and warm during the Black Death of 1348

6

☞

Medieval people

A rich baroness looking after a castle whilst her husband is at war

Archbishop Thomas Becket. He was murdered by the King's men at Canterbury Cathedral in 1170

A peasant working in the fields. Throughout the Middle Ages most people in England were peasants

Sir Simon de Montfort. He was a powerful baron and soldier

6

Clothing and equipment

Match these items to the eight people on pages 2 and 3.

crown	bible	shield	hood
sword	orb	gloves	helmet
mitre	sickle	crozier	plough
hat	apron	necklace	thread
sceptre	headdress	candle	shoes
headwrap	baby	keys	wimple

☛

Your task 💬 ✏️
Answer these questions about the eight medieval people. You might want to discuss some of them with your teacher first.

1. Why do you think the king wears a crown?

_____

2. Why do you think the archbishop holds a stick in the shape of a shepherd's crook?

_____

3. Why would a baron need a sword and shield?

_____

4. Why is the archbishop's hat bigger than a peasant's hat?

_____

5. Why do you think we know the names of lots of men from the Middle Ages but only a few women?

_____

6. Why would the nun wear clothes that were dull and dark?

_____

7. Why do you think the baroness has a set of keys to put around her waist?

_____

8. Why do the peasant man and woman wear such plain, hard-wearing clothes?

_____

9. Why does the peasant have a sickle?

_____

☞

Who was most rich and powerful in the Middle Ages?

most powerful and rich

Your task 1 🖊

Look at the diagram on the right. In the eight spaces write a description or make a simple drawing of each person you have been studying. At the top of the pyramid put the people you think were rich and powerful. At the bottom put the people whom you think were poor and not very powerful.

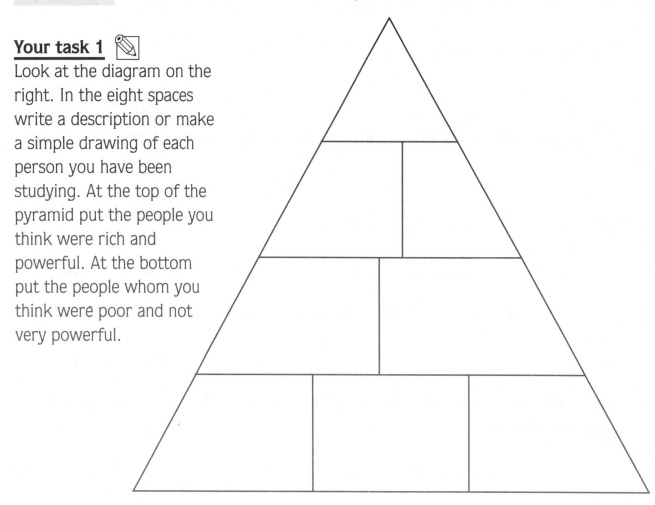

least powerful and very poor

Your task 2 🖊

Now give your reasons for putting the people in the spaces you did. Copy out the following explanation, but fill in the gaps with your own ideas. You can write as much or as little as you like.

I think the _____ was the most powerful because _____

_____ . Another reason is _____

_____

The three people whom I think had no power and were very poor are _____

_____

My reasons for choosing them are _____

7

Medieval buildings

You will need
- pen or pencil
- scissors

Your task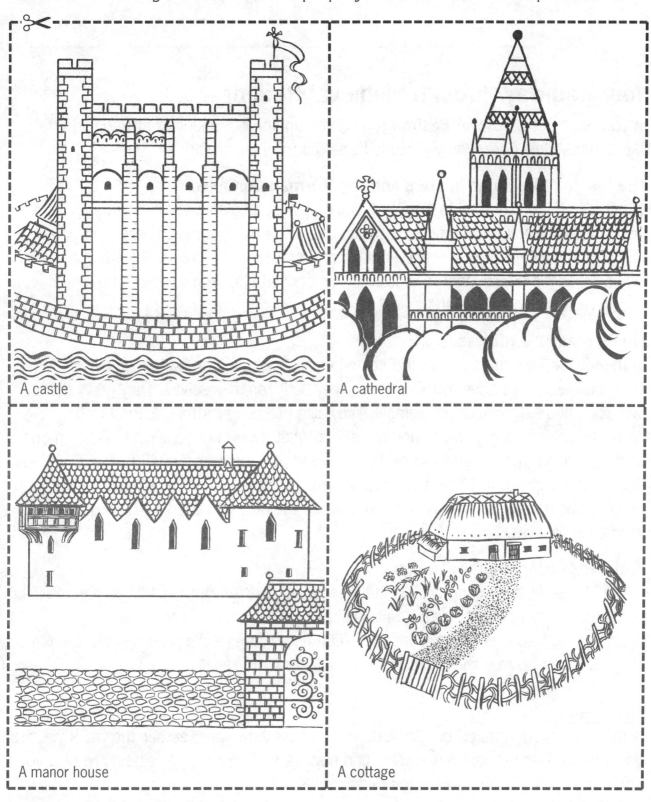

Match these buildings with some of the people you learned about in the previous task.

A castle

A cathedral

A manor house

A cottage

8

There are two pages to this task

oooooooooooooooooooooooooooooooooooooooooooooooooooooooo

You will need
- pen or pencil

◆ **HISTORY DICTIONARY**

The important words	My explanation of them
Medieval Realms	_____
	_____
	_____

Your pathway through Medieval Realms

In your study of **Medieval Realms** you will be finding out about what England was like in the Middle Ages. You will study three things in particular:

The Battle of Hastings in 1066 and the Norman Conquest

1066 is an important date in English history because England was invaded and got a new king, William of Normandy. He began to change many things. In this unit you will find out why he wanted to invade England and how he did it. You will learn about the way he changed the country so that everyone obeyed him. You will learn how he built strong castles all over England.

Life in medieval villages

In the Middle Ages most people in England were peasants who lived in small villages. Their houses were simple cottages which they built for themselves. They grew their own food and kept their own animals. They also had to work for the local lord.

In this unit you are going to find out about what it was like to live and work in one of these villages in the Middle Ages. You will find out about an awful disease, the Black Death, which spread in 1348 and killed almost half the people in England. You will also find out about a bloody rebellion in 1381 when the peasants tried to force the king to improve their lives.

Problems facing medieval kings

In the Middle Ages the king of England was very powerful. But he still had a number of problems to worry about. In this unit you can find out about three of the king's problems: how to make the barons obey him; how to make the priests in the Church obey him; how to stop the peasants in the villages from rebelling.

Your task

Using your 'route planner' on the next page discuss with your teacher the work you are going to do over the next few weeks, and how each piece of work is going to help you find out more about England in the Middle Ages.

My pathway through Medieval Realms

Name _____

Term _____

Subjects to be investigated	Date completed
Theme: _____	_____
1. _____	_____
2. _____	_____
3. _____	_____
Theme: _____	_____
1. _____	_____
2. _____	_____
3. _____	_____
Theme: _____	_____
1. _____	_____
2. _____	_____
3. _____	_____

9

There are two pages to this task

○○

You will need
• pen or pencil

◆ **HISTORY DICTIONARY**
_____

The important words   **My explanation of them**

invasion   _____

                                 _____

From across the water...

Your task

Read this description and you will begin to find out why 1066 is such an important date.

The month is September, the year is 1066. It is early in the morning, about six o'clock.

A boy and girl sit near the ruins of the old Roman fort at Pevensey on the south coast of England. For a few moments they have escaped their daily jobs.

After milking the family cow and eating a breakfast of warm milk and hard black bread they have crept away to their favourite place on the cliffs, to watch the dawn over the sea. It is getting lighter now so they can see the beach and the sea. The strong wind coming off the sea makes them shiver.

They are just about to leave when the girl notices some strange shapes on the horizon. What can they be? As the light grows stronger the shapes become clearer. They are ships, hundreds of them, and the wind is sending them towards the beach.

Without knowing it the girl and boy are seeing the beginning of one of the most important events in English history: an **invasion** which would change the lives of almost every person in England, including the lives of this boy and girl.

9

☞

King Edward's fault?

Many people would say that this invasion was all King Edward's fault. See what you think!

Edward was a weak king. One powerful English family (which was led by Harold Godwineson, Earl of Wessex) was always causing trouble for Edward. It got so bad that Edward had to ask for help from his French cousin William, Duke of Normandy. As a reward Edward promised William that he would be the next king of England. This made Harold of Wessex very angry. He was Edward's brother-in-law. He thought he should be king when Edward died.

Of course none of this would have mattered if Edward had had a son who could become king after him – but he didn't.

In January 1066 Edward died. Harold quickly made himself king. He expected trouble from William. But to start with the trouble came from somewhere else. In September Harold Hardraada, King of Norway, landed in the north of England from Norway. Hardraada also wanted to be king of England.

You can see from the map why Harold of Wessex was so worried. He had to march his army north to fight Hardraada. While he was doing this William and his Norman soldiers were sailing towards England. Harold had no army on the south coast to stop the Norman soldiers landing.

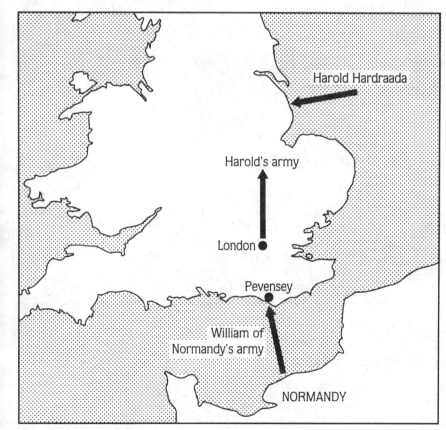

Harold did defeat Hardraada. But he then had to march his army hundreds of miles south to fight William. William's army had landed safely and had a long rest waiting for Harold's tired army to arrive.

The two sides finally met on 14 October 1066 at the Battle of Hastings.

Now you know the story, see if you can work through the following tasks.

What was happening in September 1066?

You will need

- pen or pencil
- Picture Source 2

♦ **HISTORY DICTIONARY**

The important words	My explanation of them
conqueror	_____
Norman	_____

The Battle of Hastings in 1066

The Battle of Hastings is the most famous battle in English history. It happened over 900 years ago. An English king, Harold, died in the battle. Harold's English army was beaten by a **Norman** army led by Duke William of Normandy. This meant that England got a foreign king. He became known as William the **Conqueror**.

Some of the places you will learn about have been marked on the map.

Your task

1. Put the names of the two enemies in the correct boxes on the map.

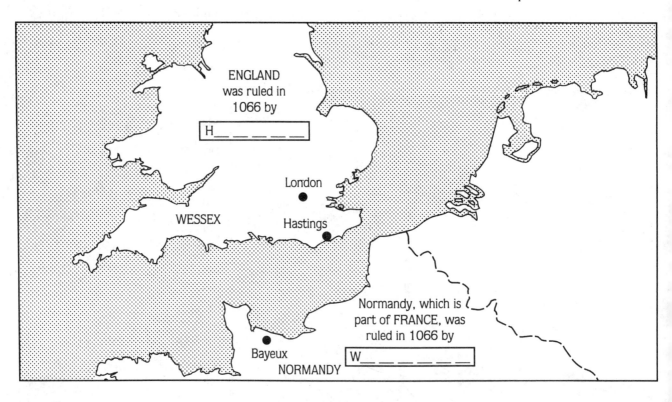

ENGLAND was ruled in 1066 by

H_ _ _ _ _ _

London

WESSEX

Hastings

Normandy, which is part of FRANCE, was ruled in 1066 by

W_ _ _ _ _ _

Bayeux

NORMANDY

2. England is part of the British Isles. It is surrounded by the sea. Why would this make it difficult for enemies to attack England?

_____

_____

10

☞

Preparing for the battle

William's army had to travel to England by boat. What things would they have to take with them?

Your task

1. Look at Picture Source 2 from the Picture Pack. This shows the Normans preparing to sail to England. In the table below list the items the Normans are taking with them. Write a sentence alongside each entry to explain how it would help the Normans to win the battle.

Item	How it would help the Normans win the battle
1.	
2.	
3.	
4.	
5.	

2. What else would the Normans need to take with them? Explain why it would be important to take each thing.

_____

_____

_____

_____

_____

_____

_____

11

You will need
- scissors
- glue

The story of the Battle of Hastings

The boxes below tell the story of the Battle of Hastings in words. On page 2 you can find the same story in pictures.

However, Ernest Muddle, a confused young man, has put the parts of the story in the wrong order. It is your task to match captions to pictures and to put them into the correct order. See if you can clear up the mess Ernest has made!

Your task

1. Cut out the pictures and the captions below and on page 2.
2. Match the captions to the pictures.
3. Put the story into chronological order.
4. When you are sure the story is in the right order, paste the cards on to a sheet of paper. They will look like a comic strip!

King Edward was King of England. He had no children. He said that William, Duke of Normandy, should be the next king.	The day after King Edward died, Harold said that he was king.	King Harold and his army met William and his army at Hastings. They fought all day.
Harold of Wessex had to march north to fight Harold Hardraada who had landed with an army.	This made William very angry with Harold. 'I will kill him,' he said.	King Harold was hit in the eye with an arrow. He died soon afterwards.
King Edward died. It was January 1066.	On 27 September 1066 William sailed from Normandy to England with a huge army.	William was pleased. He said, 'I am King of England now. I am William the Conqueror!'

The story of the Battle of Hastings: pictures

Match each of these pictures with a caption from the previous page.

12

You will need

• pen or pencil

Why was there a 'Battle of Hastings' in 1066?

There were many reasons why William and Harold fought at the Battle of Hastings in 1066. Ernest Muddle has written a list of reasons why there was a battle – but are they all correct?

Your task

1. Read the story of the Battle of Hastings again, using the comic strip you have just made.

2. Look at Ernest Muddle's list of reasons for the Battle of Hastings. Do you agree that they are all reasons why there was a battle? Put a tick next to the statements which you agree were reasons for the battle. Put a cross next to those things which you do not think were reasons why there was a battle.

Reasons why there was a 'Battle of Hastings' in 1066	✓ or ✗
■ King Edward had chosen a Frenchman, Duke William, to become King of England after he died	
■ King Edward died without a son	
■ Harold always had three 'Shredded Wheat' for breakfast	
■ Harold became King of England instead of Duke William	
■ Duke William built lots of castles	
■ Duke William wanted to become King of England	
■ Duke William landed in England with a very strong army	
■ After the battle a tapestry was made which told the story of the Norman invasion and the Battle of Hastings	

12

page 2

Your task

You are going to write an essay with the title 'Why was there a Battle of Hastings?' Part of the essay has been written for you. Copy it out and see if you can fill in the gaps using the reasons for the battle which you marked on the last page.

Why was there a Battle of Hastings?

The Battle of Hastings happened because two men both thought they should be the next king of England after Edward died.

William thought he should be king because _____

_____

_____

_____ .

Harold of Wessex thought he should be king because _____

_____

_____

_____ .

There might not have been a battle at all if Edward had _____

_____

_____ .

After Edward's death Harold made William angry by _____

_____

_____

_____ .

The final reason why there was a battle was because William's army ____

_____

_____

_____

_____ .

13

There are two pages to this task

ooooooooooooooooooooooooooooooooooooooooooooooooooooooooo

You will need
- pen or pencil

◆ **HISTORY DICTIONARY**

The important words	My explanation of them
bias	_____
	_____

The Battle of Hastings: examining the evidence

Many of the historical sources that we use to investigate the Battle of Hastings were written or made hundreds of years ago. Some of them were written by people on William's side. Some were written by people on Harold's side.

Some sources are **biased** towards the French soldiers and their leader William. Some sources are biased towards the English soldiers and their leader Harold. On the next page are two sources about the battle. You are going to decide which way each one is biased.

Your task

1. Read Source 1. Underline all the words or phrases which show that William was a clever and a brave leader and that Harold was not brave.
2. Read Source 2. Underline all the words or phrases which show that Harold was brave and that William was not brave.
3. One of these accounts was a written by a Norman who worked for William, the other was written by English monks. Which do you think is which?

Source ____ was written by a Norman.

The reason I think this is _____

_____

_____

_____

Source ____ was written by English monks.

The reason I think this is _____

_____

_____

_____

☞

Two sources for the battle

SOURCE 1 This story of the battle is based on an account written by William of Poitiers

1. William's army advanced steadily. They were well organised. The crossbowmen were at the front. Next came soldiers on foot, then at the back, knights on horseback.

2. Harold's army was much larger than William's. He was scared to fight on equal terms, so he put his army at the top of a hill.

3. The Norman soldiers attacked but were pushed back down the hill by the English who had more soldiers.

4. William's bravery made the Normans forget their fear and they attacked again. William then told them to pretend to run away. The English chased after them down the hill. William then ordered his knights to turn their horses round and attack the English. They could now cut them down easily.

SOURCE 2 This story of the battle is rather different from Source 1

1. William attacked the English before they were ready for battle. The English army did not have enough space in which to fight properly.

2. The English soldiers began to desert Harold and run away.

3. Harold fought bravely all day. The Normans were not winning. But then Harold was killed and this meant the Normans had won.

14

The Battle of Hastings: your own version

You have studied different evidence about the Battle of Hastings. Use everything you have learned to do the following task.

Your task

You are either an English or a Norman soldier who has survived the battle. Tell the story of the battle from your point of view.

✥ *December 1066. Three months after the battle at Hastings* ✥

An account as witnessed by _____

_____

_____

_____

_____

_____

_____

_____

_____

_____

_____

signed _____

member of the _____ army and

forever loyal to King _____

15

Why did William win the Battle of Hastings?

Your task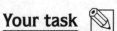

On the right-hand side of this page Ernest Muddle has written down a list of reasons why William won the Battle of Hastings. But some of them are not reasons at all. Draw a line from the question on the left to any real reasons.

Why did William win the Battle of Hastings?

William wanted to be king of England.

Harold's army was tired after marching all the way from the north. William's army was fresh and ready to fight.

Harold was killed in the battle. This made the English give up because they had lost their leader.

Harold wanted to be king of England.

William's soldiers tricked the English army by pretending to run away.

The Normans were better armed than the English.

The English army was larger than the Norman army.

Edward had promised William that he would be the next king of England.

16

There are four pages to this task

You will need

- pen or pencil
- crayons

How did William gain control?

William the Conqueror had many problems to solve after he became king, as you can see from the picture below.

William's problems

A
Some of King Harold's army are still in London. These men do not like me. They are angry that Harold is dead.

B
This is a big country. My spies tell me that the Danes are plotting with the Englishmen. They might come south to try to take over the whole country.

C
There are English soldiers in a castle in Dover. They might attack all the men in my army.

☞

Your task

1. Read Sources 1–3 which describe some of William's solutions to his problems.
2. Match each of his problems to one of the solutions. Use this table.

Problem	Solution and its source number
A	
B	
C	

William's solutions

SOURCE 1 Written by William of Poitiers in around 1071

Then William marched to Dover which was held by a large army. The English were afraid and prepared to surrender, but our men set fire to the castle and most of it was destroyed.

SOURCE 2 Florence of Worcester describes what William was doing before he went to London

William laid waste Sussex, Kent, Hampshire and Surrey, and slaughtered many people who lived there. He was then met by Londoners who gave in to him.

SOURCE 3 Written by a monk trained in Normandy

The King's army approached York only to find out that the Danes had fled. The King was angry. He killed many people and burned down the homes of others. As a result of this there was a terrible famine. More than 100,000 Christian folk died of hunger.

☞

Your task 🖉
Choose one of William's solutions from page 2, and draw a picture showing what he did. Then write a caption for it.

This drawing shows William _____

_____

16

William's solutions

These sources from pages 78–79 of *Contrasts and Connections* will give you more information for your drawings.

SOURCE 1 Written by William of Poitiers in around 1071. He fought for William of Normandy

Then William marched to Dover, which was held by a large force. The English were stricken with fear and prepared to surrender unconditionally, but our men, greedy for booty, set fire to the castle and the greater part of it was destroyed. The Duke, unwilling that those who had offered to surrender should suffer loss, gave them money for the damage. Having taken possession of the castle, the Duke spent eight days adding new fortifications to it.

SOURCE 2 Florence of Worcester describing William's movements before he went to London

Earl William was laying waste Sussex, Kent, Hampshire, Surrey, Middlesex and Hertfordshire and ceased not from burning villages and slaughtering the inhabitants. He was then met by the Earls Edwin and Morcar and Londoners of the better sort, who submitted to him.

SOURCE 3 Written about 60 years after the events described, by a monk trained in Normandy

The royal forces approached York, only to learn that the Danes had fled. The King ordered his men to repair the castles in the city. He himself continued to comb forests and remote mountainous places, stopping at nothing to hunt out the enemy hidden there. He cut down many in his vengeance; destroyed the lairs of others; harried the land, and burned homes to ashes. Nowhere else had William shown such cruelty. He made no effort to control his fury and punished the innocent with the guilty. In his anger he ordered that all crops, herds and food of every kind should be brought together and burned to ashes, so that the whole region north of the Humber might be stripped of all means of sustenance. As a result of this such a terrible famine fell upon the humble and defenceless people that more than 100,000 Christian folk of both sexes, young and old alike, perished of hunger.

SOURCE 4 Florence of Worcester describing conditions about twenty years after the Conquest

So severe was the famine in most parts of the kingdom, that men were driven to feed on the flesh of horses, dogs, cats and even of human beings.

☞

Your task
Use what you have found out about William's problems and solutions to complete this essay on how William defeated his enemies.

How William defeated his enemies

Before William could conquer other parts of the country he first had to defeat the

English soldiers at Dover. He _____

_____

_____

_____

_____

William then went to _____

Here he _____

_____

_____ . The city of _____ then gave in to him.

William's biggest problem was in the North of England where the Danes were

helping the English. What William did was very cruel. He _____

_____

_____

_____

_____

_____

You will need
- pen or pencil

♦ HISTORY DICTIONARY

The important words	My explanation of them
lords and barons	_____
knights	_____
taxes	_____

How did William keep control?

William became King of England. But not everyone obeyed him. Many English **lords** and **barons** did not want him to be king. William could not trust them to obey him. They might even persuade the people in their area to fight against him.

Imagine you are an advisor to King William. Can you advise him how to control the people of England?

Your task

1. Here are five things which William could do to control the people of England. Read them carefully.
2. Decide which two are best.
3. On page 3 write a letter to King William telling him what to do.

A
Take the land away from the English barons. Give some of it to your friends, the Norman barons. Keep most of it yourself.

B
Make a huge army to frighten everybody. Force the English knights to join your army.

C
Build strong castles all over England. Put your Norman barons in charge of them.

D
Make the people pay taxes to pay for your army. You will first have to find out how much money and possessions people have got.

E
Make laws. If people break these laws, your friends the Norman barons will fine them or punish them.

☛

Letter to King William

Use this page to write your letter to King William.

Dear King William,

My advice to you concerning keeping control of these dreadful Englishmen who hate you so much is

1.

_____

_____

_____

_____

2.

_____

_____

_____

_____

Your loyal subject

_____

18

You will need
- pen or pencil

◆ **HISTORY DICTIONARY**

The important words	My explanation of them
survey	_____
doomsday	_____
Domesday Book	_____

The Domesday Book

King William decided that one of the best ways to keep control in England was to find out what people owned and to make them pay taxes.

In 1086 William sent his knights to every single village in the country to do a **survey**. He told the knights to find out what each person owned and to threaten to kill people if they would not tell them.

The people were so scared that they thought it was their '**doomsday**'. William asked the knights to record everything they found out in a huge book. This became known as the **Domesday Book**.

18

☞ Look at the diagram on the next page which is about the survey in the village of Elton. You can see what William's men asked about. You can also find out some of the answers they received.

Your task 📖✏️

1. In the first column of the table below complete the list of things that King William's men asked about the village of Elton.
2. In the second column write the information they found out.

King William's officials asked	The answers they got
a) What is the village called?	
b) How many ploughs are there?	
c)	
d)	
e)	
f)	
g)	

The Domesday survey

The King's officials met the priest, the reeve and six men from each village. The King's men asked:

what the manor (the village) was called

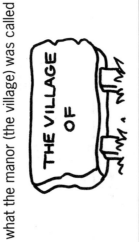

THE VILLAGE OF

Answer
Elton

how much land there was in the village

Answer
10 hides (=1200 acres)

how many ploughs there were

Answer   The Lord has 4 ploughs.
The villagers have 20 ploughs.

how many mills there were

Mills were where
the grain was
made into flour

Answer
2 mills

how many villagers there were

Answer
28 villagers and a priest

how much woodland there was

Answer
(no answer recorded)

The villagers grazed their sheep
and goats in the meadows

how much meadow there was

Answer
170 acres

18

☞

The Domesday Survey

Your task

1. Look at the questions William's men asked. Why do you think King William wanted to know these things?

_____

_____

_____

_____

_____

2. Why do you think he wrote down all the information in the Domesday Book?

_____

_____

_____

_____

_____

_____

19

Castles

You will need

- pen or pencil

King William liked castles. As he said, 'Castles are safe and strong. No one can attack me if I build castles.'

He built his first castle at Hastings very soon after winning the Battle of Hastings. At first he built wooden castles which only took a few weeks to make. Later on he built stone castles which took much longer.

Your task ✎

Look at the picture below, which shows one of William's first 'wooden' castles, and label the castle and the hill on which it stands.

C&C pp. 82–83 *MEDIEVAL REALMS SUPPORT MATERIALS*

☞

Your task
Look back at the picture on the previous page. It shows the kind of castle that William built to start with.

1. What are the two men on horseback holding?

_____

_____

_____

2. How can you tell that the castle is made of wood?

_____

_____

_____

_____

3. How many men are attacking the castle?

_____

4. How many men are defending the castle?

_____

5. Two men are trying to set fire to the castle. Colour them in.

6. One man inside the castle is trying to help the attackers. Which one? Colour him in.

7. How is he trying to help them?

_____

_____

_____

_____

_____

20

You will need

- scissors
- glue

The Castle Challenge

One of the most important things King William did to take control of England was to build strong castles.

As you complete your work on this section of the unit you will put together your own picture of a strong Norman castle.

Your task 1

Each time you complete a piece of work, your teacher will give you some more pieces to add to your castle. This is what the finished castle should look like:

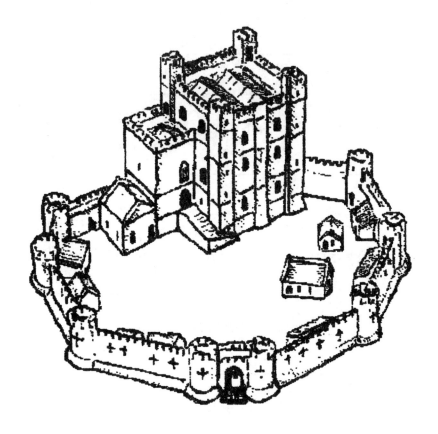

Your task 2

When the castle is finished, fill it with people who lived in it and soldiers who guarded it. You could copy these figures:

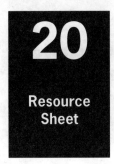

Castle components for Task 20 (the Castle Challenge)

1. Photocopy this sheet on to thick paper or card, one per pupil, enlarged if necessary.
2. Give the components out in the order shown.

1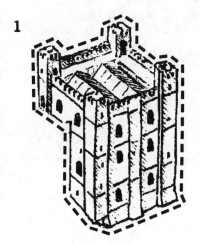

4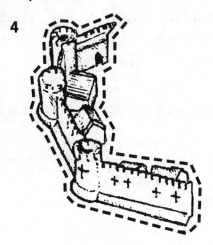

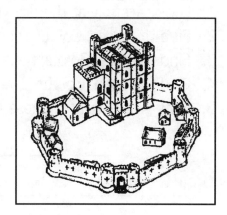

2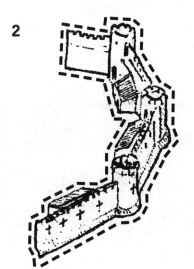

5

3

6

7

21

You will need

- pen or pencil
- crayons

Where would you build your castle?

Before you start to build a castle you must decide where to put it.

Your task

1. Look carefully at the drawing on the next page. Find the river. Colour it blue.
2. Find the trees. Colour them brown.
3. Find the hills. Colour them grey.
4. Find the road. Colour it yellow.
5. How would each of these features be useful to a castle builder?

The river _____

_____

_____

The trees _____

_____

_____

The hills _____

_____

_____

The road _____

_____

_____

Where would you build your castle?

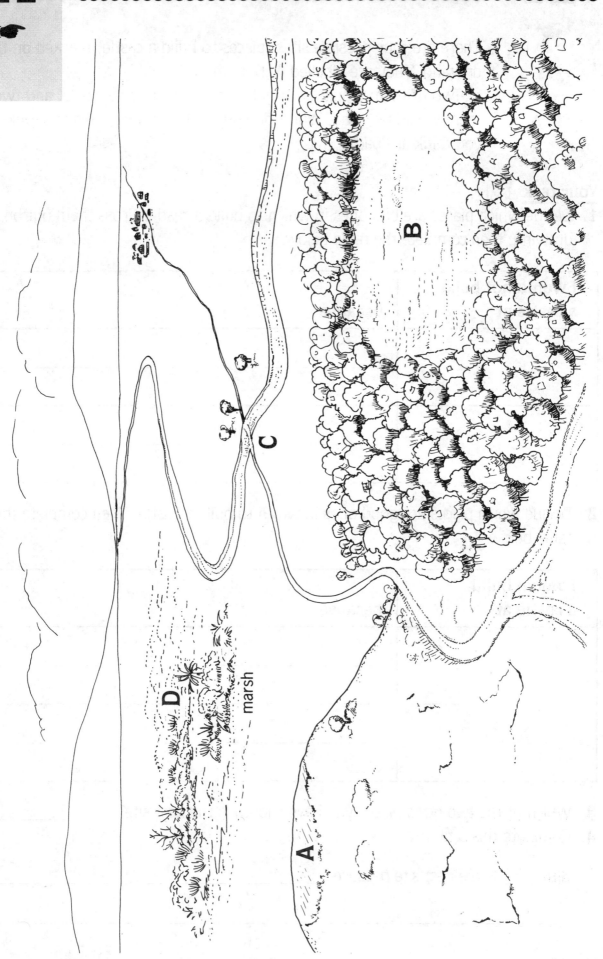

marsh

A

B

C

D

There are four possible sites (places to build a castle) marked on the drawing. They are labelled A, B, C and D.

Two of them would be very bad places to build a castle, and two of them would be good. Which do you think are good sites and which do you think are bad?

Your task ✎

1. Decide which places are bad ones in which to build a castle. Cross them out on your drawing, then complete the table below.

I would not build a castle at	because

2. Decide which places are good ones in which to build a castle. Then complete the table below.

I would build a castle at	because

3. Which of the two good places you have chosen is the best site? _____

4. Complete this sentence:

   Site _____ is the best site because _____

   _____

   _____

22

There are two pages to this task

∞∞

You will need
- pen or pencil
- crayons

Features of a castle

A castle had two main uses. In times of war it could defend you and your soldiers from being attacked. In times of peace it was a place for you and your family to live as comfortably as you could.

So your castle needed to be strong enough to protect you from attack but it also needed to be a nice place to live.

Here are some possible features of a castle:

thick, strong walls	☐
made of wood	☐
surrounded by a thick forest	☐
narrow windows	☐
strong wooden doors	☐
wide windows	☐
gaps in the walls instead of doors	☐
surrounded by a moat filled with water	☐
short towers	☐
made of stone	☐
thin walls	☐
high towers	☐

Your task

1. Put a tick by the features that you would like your castle to have, and a cross by the ones you would not like it to have.

2. On the next page complete the description of your castle to include some of the features you have chosen. Draw a picture of it in the box below.

22

☞

⦾⦾

My ideal castle

Complete this description of your ideal castle and draw it in the box below. Include in your description some of the features you chose on the previous page.

I would choose _____ walls for my castle.

I would choose _____ towers for my castle.

I would build my castle out of _____

The entrance to my castle would be _____

_____

The windows of my castle would be _____

_____

I would surround my castle with a _____

_____

23

You will need
- pen or pencil

◆ **HISTORY DICTIONARY**

The important words	My explanation of them
feudal system	_____
	_____

The feudal system

The **feudal system** was set up by William as a way of controlling England.

King William owned most of the land in England.

He gave much of it to people (lords) who were loyal to him. In return they paid William money and provided him with soldiers for his army when he needed them.

300 soldiers

The lords allowed the peasants to use some of their land. In return the peasants had to work on the lord's farmland when he wanted them to, pay him rent, and give him some of the food that they produced.

24

There are four pages to this task

○○

You will need
• pen or pencil

♦ HISTORY DICTIONARY

The important words	My explanation of them
archaeologist	_____
	_____

The lost village of Wharram Percy in Yorkshire

In the Middle Ages nearly everyone lived in the country. Some people lived in small villages, and others in much larger ones.

Most people lived in cottages made out of wood and wattle and daub. Wattle was sticks which were woven together to make a wall. Daub was mud or clay which was then plastered on to the wattle. The cottages had thatched roofs made of straw.

Part of the house was used for keeping animals or storing crops. These little cottages used to get damp and rotten when it rained. If they weren't looked after properly, they fell down.

A few rich people such as the lord of the manor or the priest lived in stone houses. These were usually a lot bigger than the peasants' cottages, and had a separate area for keeping animals and storing crops.

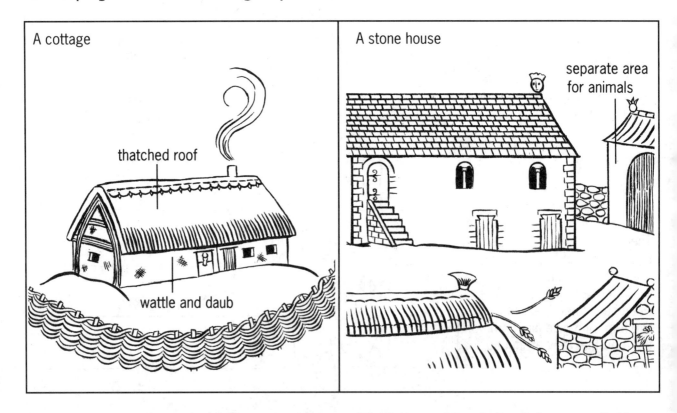

A cottage — thatched roof — wattle and daub

A stone house — separate area for animals

Many of these villages have disappeared now. There is nothing left of them at all. You need to be a very good history detective to work out what they once looked like.

24

☞

Archaeological evidence

One way of finding out about medieval villages is to look for archaeological evidence – which means any objects or parts of buildings that are left in the ground. The person who looks for this kind of evidence is called an **archaeologist**.

Look at the photograph on page 3. It was taken from inside an aeroplane. Archaeologists think that this used to be a village in the Middle Ages, called Wharram Percy. They think the square shapes show where cottages used to be.

Your task 🖉

1. On your own copy of the photograph mark each of the cottages. The first one has been done for you.

2. How many cottages can you find?

_____

3. Why do you think there is nothing left of the cottages? (You may need to look back at the information on the previous page for clues.)

_____

_____

_____

4. What do you think the long thin lines (marked [1]) on the photograph are?

_____

_____

_____

5. What do you think the bumps in the ground (marked [2]) might be?

_____

_____

_____

_____

☛ Aerial photograph of Wharram Percy

●●

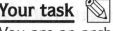

Archaeologist's report on Wharram Percy

Your task

You are an archaeologist who has just received the aerial photograph
of Wharram Percy. Complete this report.

Date: _____

From the evidence of _____

it is clear that there is a _____

in this area.

Seen from the air, the uneven ground shows signs of:

1. _____

_____

2. _____

_____

There are _____ buildings still standing.

One of these is _____

I therefore conclude that it would be valuable to investigate this village

further to help us understand how people lived in the Middle Ages.

Signed _____

(Archaeologist)

ARCHAEOLOGICAL UNIT

25

You will need
- pen or pencil

♦ **HISTORY DICTIONARY**

The important words	My explanation of them
baptism	_____
	_____

Alice's Unhappy Day

Hundreds of years ago a girl called Alice lived in the village of Wharram Percy. In this story Alice is getting ready for an important day – the baptism of her new baby brother.

Your task

1. Read the story and find out what happens to Alice.
2. Read the story again, and this time circle the places Alice visits and mark her route on the plan of the village on page 4.

Story

Alice woke up. Her house was right next door to the church and the bells were ringing. It was Sunday morning. Alice yawned.

Suddenly Alice remembered. Today was a special day. Walter, her new baby brother, was going to be baptised.

Where are my mother and father?

Alice remembered it was a special day. Walter was going to be baptised

☞   She hurried to get dressed. 'Mother and Father never usually let me sleep in, she said to herself. 'Mother,' she called. There was no reply. 'Where are they?' she wondered.

She looked around. The cottage was deserted. The fire had not been lit. No water had been boiled in the pot. The straw on the floor had not been changed. The ham was still hooked up on the ceiling. It should have been roasting in the pot ready for the celebration. Now Alice was getting worried.

She ran out of the door and called out, 'Mother! Father!' No one replied.

She ran across the track to the cottage where her cousin Elizabeth lived. But Elizabeth was not there. The goats and the pigs were still inside the cottage. Normally Elizabeth let them out as soon as the sun rose.

What was wrong? Alice tried not to panic. She ran past the church, shouting for her mother and father. Behind the church was the priest's house. She knocked on the door. A servant shouted through the window.

'He must be in the church getting ready for the baptism. Don't you hear the bells? You should be there too!'

Alice ran back to the church. Almost everyone in the village was there, except the priest. And there was no sign of her mother and father.

That was enough for poor Alice! In tears she ran down the path, past her own house and right up to the far end of the village. Her best friend Sarah lived there. Once they had counted how many other houses there were between Sarah's and Alice's houses. There were twelve.

Alice ran to her best friend Sarah's house at the other end of the village

Alice ran into Sarah's house. She did not even knock at the door. Sarah's mother was just fastening her shawl with a pretty new brooch. Sarah was tying a strip of leather to the end of her long plait.

'Whatever is the matter, young Alice?' asked Sarah's mother. 'Why aren't you getting ready for the christening?'

'Mother, Father and baby Walter have all gone,' cried Alice. 'Elizabeth has gone too. People are in church waiting for the christening to begin.'

25

☞ 'Dear God,' said Sarah's mother. 'The baby must be ill. Come quickly. Let us see if your mother has taken him to the wise woman.'

The wise woman lived in the cottage at the back of the manor house, just behind the dovecote. Quickly Alice, Sarah and her mother ran across the track, over the grass and down the muddy path behind the houses.

People in their Sunday best passed them and waved. 'See you in church, Alice,' they shouted. 'Hope your mother has a good feast laid on?'

Alice, Sarah and her mother arrived at the wise woman's house. A strong smell of willow herb and lavender came from the fire in the centre of the room. There stood Mother and Father. Mother held baby Walter in her arms. She was crying. Walter looked stiff and white. Elizabeth and the priest were there too.

The wise woman put her arms around Alice.

'There will be no feast today, my child,' she said. 'Your baby brother became ill in the night. We tried everything to save him. I tried all my herbs and lotions. We even put a cat's paw on his chest whilst I chanted my best spell. But God has taken him away from us. He has gone.'

Alice found her mother and father in the wise woman's house

'He has died, just like your sister Emma and your brothers John and Andrew,' cried Alice's mother.

'But was he christened?' asked Sarah's mother. 'Yes, he was,' said the priest, 'just before he breathed his last'.

Sarah's mother looked relieved. But Father's face was stern and sad. They had had five babies but only Alice was still alive.

Alice looked at her mother. Why did God treat them like this?

Was it because Alice had not said her prayers the night before?

Was it because Father had forgotten to pay his taxes to the priest?

Was it because Mother was so tired from working in the fields that she did not have enough milk to feed baby Walter?

No one would ever know.

So there was no celebration on that Sunday in Wharram Percy. What was to be a day of happiness became a day of sadness for Alice, her mother, her father, her cousin Elizabeth and her best friend Sarah.

MEDIEVAL REALMS SUPPORT MATERIALS

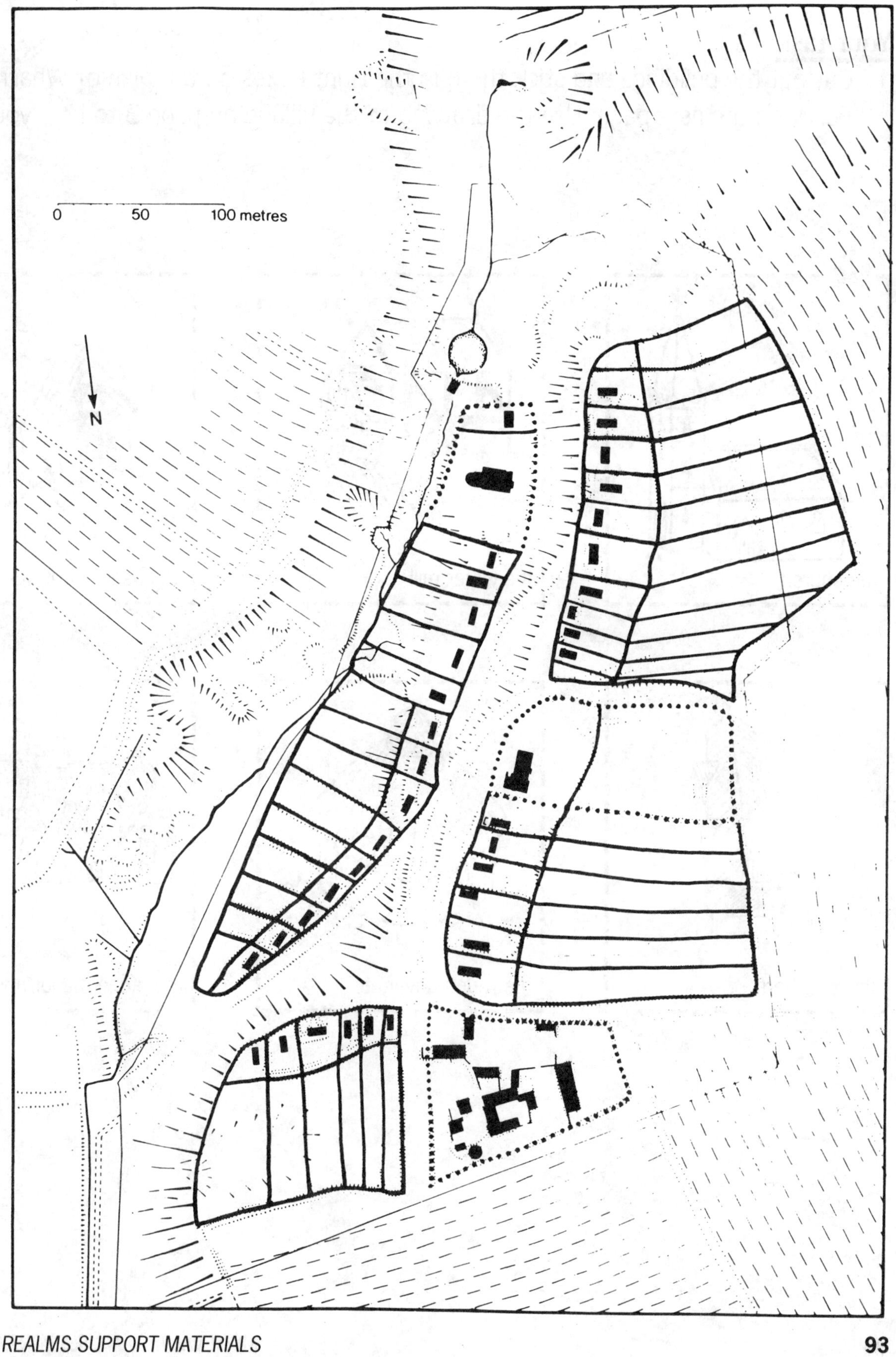

Plan of Wharram Percy

Circle the places which Alice visits and mark her route on this plan.

0   50   100 metres

N

26

You will need
- scissors
- glue

The buildings of Wharram Percy

Here are pictures of six different buildings. All these buildings were in the village of Wharram Percy.

Your task

1. Cut out the buildings and stick them in the right boxes on the plan of Wharram Percy on the next page. Use the drawing of the village on page 3 to help you.

the church

the water mill

a peasant's cottage

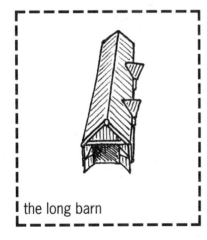

the long barn

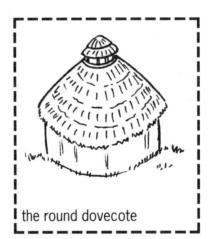

the round dovecote

the stone manor house

26

☞

A plan of Wharram Percy

Stick the buildings in the right boxes
on this plan.

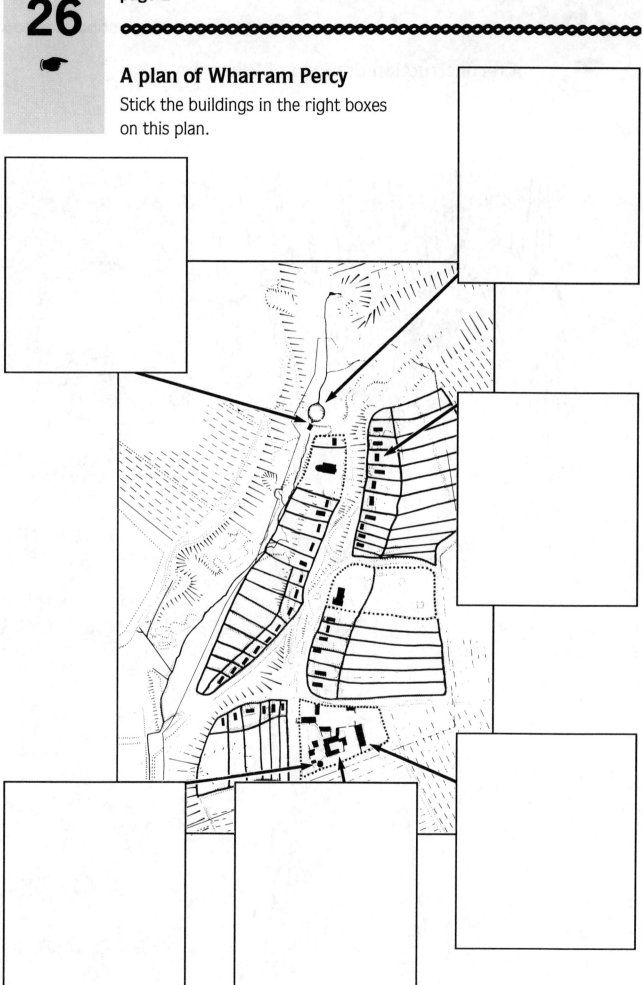

A reconstruction drawing of Wharram Percy

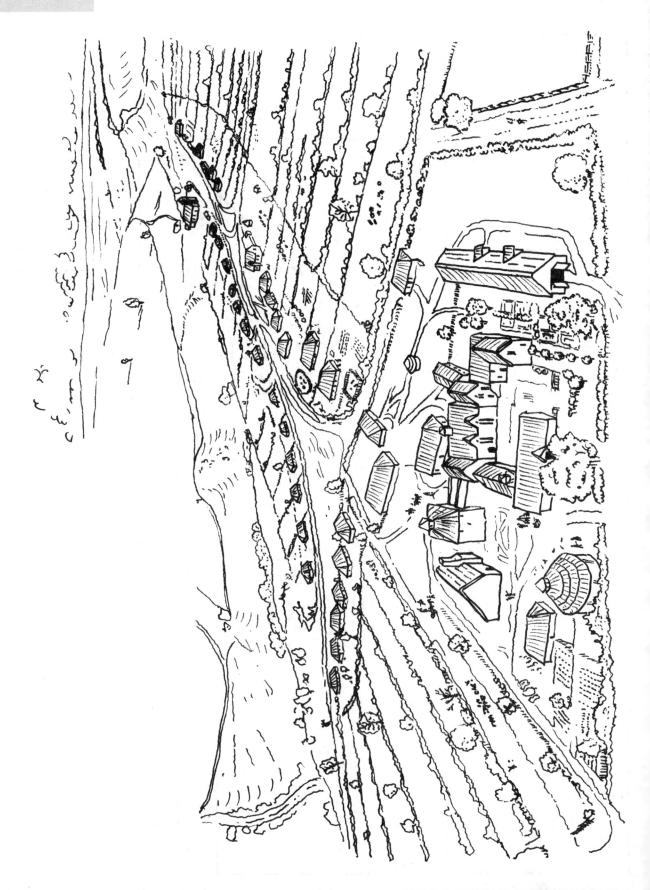

27

There are three pages to this task

You will need

- pen or pencil

The archaeology game

When archaeologists find a lost village like Wharram Percy, they dig into the soil to look for clues about the village and the people who lived in it.

They have to be very careful. When they find something buried in the soil they have to write down exactly where they found it. They therefore make a grid like the one below. You have probably used grids like this in maths or geography. They make this grid by stretching string over the soil. Then they start digging in each square, very slowly and very carefully.

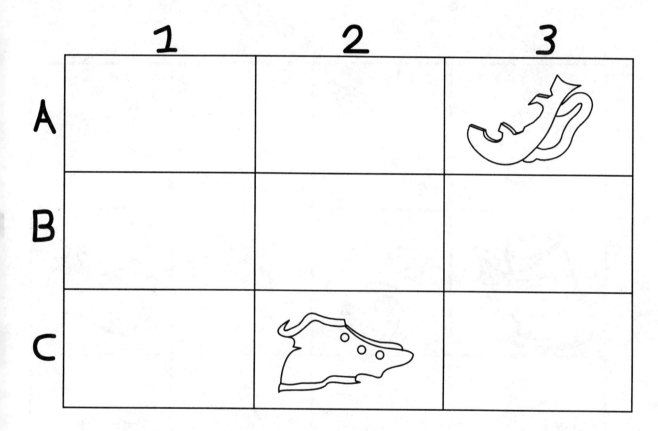

When they find an object, they write a description of it. They write the grid reference (the number and the letter) of the square it was in. For example:

Description	Grid reference
broken piece of pot	A3

Your task

Add to the table above a description and grid reference for the other object that the archaeologists have found.

MEDIEVAL REALMS SUPPORT MATERIALS

97

27

Ernest Muddle is looking for evidence from the Middle Ages. He has discovered the remains of a medieval cottage. But he has a problem. The archaeological evidence is underneath a rubbish dump at the end of someone's garden. Some of the objects he finds are from modern times. He is not sure which objects are medieval and which are modern. See if you can help him.

Your task

Cross out the objects which are not from the Middle Ages.

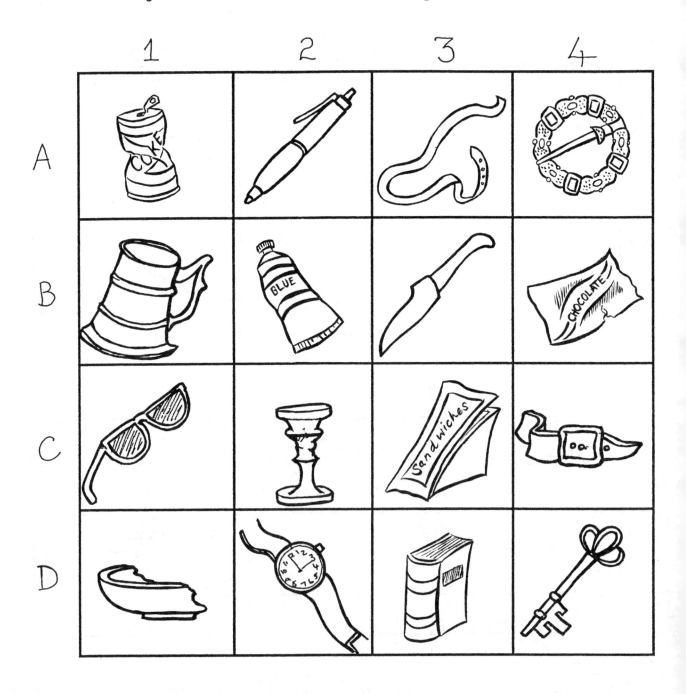

Ernest has drawn up this list of the objects which he thinks come from the Middle Ages. But he has got into a muddle and has not written down the grid references for the squares where he found them.

Your task

Complete Ernest Muddle's archaeological report by adding:

1. the grid reference for each object
2. your ideas about what it might have been used for.

Name: Ernest Muddle
Date:
Site: the medieval cottage

Object	Grid ref.	Who might have used it and what they might have used it for
■ knife		
■ silver brooch		
■ pewter tankard		
■ key		
■ broken pottery		
■ brass candlestick		
■ piece of leather belt		
■ strip of leather		

28

You will need

- pen or pencil

♦ **HISTORY DICTIONARY**

The important words	**My explanation of them**
reconstruct	_____
	_____

How can we reconstruct the village of Elton?

You have investigated one medieval village – Wharram Percy – which was deserted and where the only evidence was archaeological. The village of Elton in Cambridgeshire is quite different. People still live there today. But the medieval houses have all been knocked down, and because newer buildings now stand in the same places, an archaeologist cannot dig around for remains of the old ones.

So how can you, the historian, find out what Elton really looked like hundreds of years ago? How can you **reconstruct** the village so that you can see a picture of it in your mind? On the next page is a diagram showing the sources which are available for you to use.

I wonder what Elton looked like in the Middle Ages?

Your task

1. Look at the sources about Elton which are available, and put a circle round those which would be helpful in finding out what it looked like in the Middle Ages.
2. Cross out the sources which would not be helpful.
3. Which kind of source would be most helpful?

   _____

4. Why do you think this?

   _____

   _____

Sources about Elton

Put a circle round the helpful sources. Cross out the unhelpful sources.

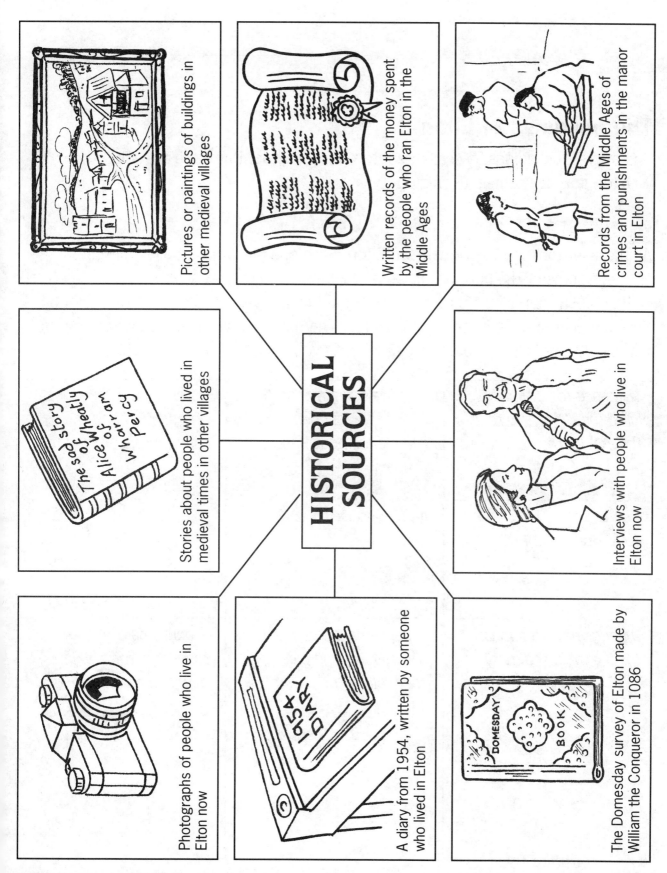

Pictures or paintings of buildings in other medieval villages

Written records of the money spent by the people who ran Elton in the Middle Ages

Records from the Middle Ages of crimes and punishments in the manor court in Elton

The sad story of Wheatly Alice of Warram Percy

Stories about people who lived in medieval times in other villages

HISTORICAL SOURCES

Interviews with people who live in Elton now

Photographs of people who live in Elton now

A diary from 1954, written by someone who lived in Elton

DOMESDAY BOOK

The Domesday survey of Elton made by William the Conqueror in 1086

29

You will need

- pen or pencil

◆ **HISTORY DICTIONARY**

The important words	My explanation of them
written sources	_____
	_____

The buildings of Elton

The medieval buildings have all disappeared from Elton. But there are still some **written sources** to help us find out what used to be there.

Your task

All these written sources come from Elton. Each one mentions a building in Elton although some of the buildings have unusual names!

Read each source carefully. In the box underneath it, write down the names of any buildings that are mentioned in the source. The first two have been done for you. If you need more help, discuss the sources with your teacher before you start.

15 pence for a thatcher hired for 20 days to thatch the stable, the dovecote and the sheepfold	*4 pence for a mason to mend the wall between the manor house and the granary*	*4 pence paid for stone bought to mend the foundations of the mills*
stable dovecote sheepfold	manor house granary	
9 pence paid to a mason for mending the dairy	*8 pence paid to a mason for making one piece of the wall of the pound*	*6 pence paid to a carpenter for making new beams for the kiln*

2 pence paid to a carpenter for mending the common privy	*20 shillings paid to carpenters for erecting and mending the dovecote next to the chapel*	*Thomas de Chauseye carried away the door posts of the house of Richard son of Ellis*
16 pence paid to one slater for mending the roof of the manor house, kitchen and bakehouse	*6 pence for a thatcher to thatch the ox shed*	*2 water mills and a fulling mill also belonged to the Abbot*
2 shillings paid to a man thatching the barn	*13 pence paid to a carpenter for work on the chapel*	

☛

On page 4 there are some pictures of medieval buildings. They come from other villages but they show buildings that were also in Elton.

Your task 📝 ✏️

1. Work out which of the buildings shown in the pictures are mentioned in your written evidence.

2. Use the written sources and the pictures to complete this table about the buildings in Elton. You can ask your teacher for extra written sources about Elton.

Type of building	What was it made of?	What was it used for?
sheepfold	branches and thatch	keeping the sheep in

☛ **Medieval buildings**

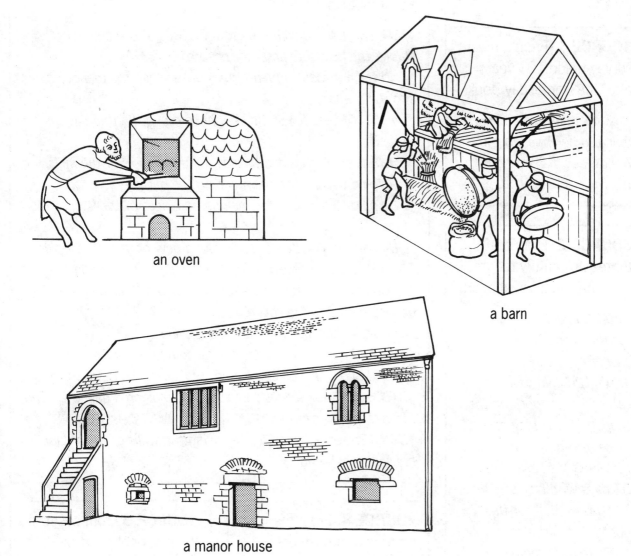

an oven

a barn

a manor house

a peasant's cottage

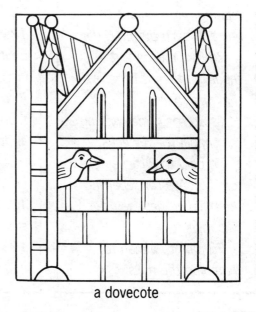

a dovecote

Further written sources about Elton

SOURCE 1 From a royal survey made 100 years after the Domesday Book

2 water mills and a fulling mill also belonged to the Abbot, also fishing rights on the river.

SOURCE 2 From the thirteenth-century records of money spent by the lord

1286 6d paid for branches for the barn and the sheepfold.

1297 12d paid to a carpenter for work on the chapel, 12 working days.

2s paid to a man thatching the barn during 32 days with board.

1d for a bolt for the door of the little barn.

6d to a carpenter for making gates before the hall and barn during 6 days.

2d to a mason for repairing the walls before the great barn.

5s 2d for 4 men slating the chapel for 3 weeks.

7d paid to 2 carpenters for 3½ days for repairing the building between the two mills.

7d paid to a man for thatching the mills.

SOURCE 3 From the fourteenth-century records of money spent by the lord of Elton

1307 15d for a thatcher hired for 20 days to thatch the stable, the dovecote and the sheepfold.

4d for a mason to mend the wall between the manor house and the granary.

1311 4d paid for stone bought to mend the foundations of the mills.

3s 8d for 38 wooden boards for the wheels of the mills.

9d paid to a mason for mending the dairy.

8d paid to a mason for making one piece of the wall of the pound.

6d paid to a carpenter for making new beams for the kiln.

1313 2d paid to a carpenter for mending the common privy.

20d paid to 2 carpenters for erecting and mending the dovecote next to the chapel.

6d for a thatcher to thatch the ox-shed.

1324 16d paid to one slater for mending the roof of the manor house, kitchen and bakehouse during 16 days with food.

1345 3s 11d for stones and slates for making a new oven and furnace in the manor.

1350 12d for a mason for repairing the walls of the manor house after the flood.

SOURCE 4 From the records of money paid to the lord of Elton

1296 22d for letting the boat from time to time.

3s 4d rent from Adam Bird for an oven, and 8s 4d from Henry the smith for another oven.

13d 9d profit from the pound.

1307 6d from Robert the smith for one smithy.

1350 40s rent for the 3 mills, 2 grist and 1 fulling.

SOURCE 5 From cases in the manorial court of Elton

1308 Thomas de Chauseye carried away the door posts of the house of Richard son of Ellis, and broke the thatch of his wall. Fine of 6d.

30

You will need

• pen or pencil

Inside a peasant's cottage

In many ways people who lived during the Middle Ages were just like you and me. They did many of the same things as people do today. They had to feed and clothe their families. They had to go to work. They got married and they looked after their children. Sometimes they quarrelled with their neighbours. Sometimes they got into trouble because they broke the law.

Other things about the Middle Ages were different from today. The houses were different, and so were the ways in which people dressed, the way they travelled and the diseases they got.

In the next few tasks you are going to use a wide range of evidence to find out what it was like to live in a medieval village.

Your task

1. On the next page there is a picture of the inside of a peasant's cottage in the Middle Ages. Match each of the four descriptions at the top with a letter on the picture and draw a line between them.
2. Add labels to describe anything else you can see in the picture.
3. The picture tells us some things about life in a medieval village but not everything. Here are some descriptions of what life was like for peasants in the Middle Ages. Put a tick if the description matches what is shown in the picture. Put a cross if it does not match.

Description	✓	✗
■ Life for the peasants was miserable.	☐	
■ They only had one room to live in.	☐	
■ There was no light in the room.	☐	
■ The floor was covered with rushes and straw.	☐	
■ Rubbish collected and rotted away among the rushes and straw.	☐	
■ In the middle of the room there was a fire.	☐	
■ It was very smoky inside the room.	☐	
■ Animals were kept in the same building that the people lived in.	☐	
■ There was never any time for sport or entertainment.	☐	
■ People ate only bread and cheese.	☐	

Inside a peasant's cottage

Draw lines to connect the descriptions with the correct letter on the picture.

cows	spinning	meat hanging up	cooking

31

You will need

- pen or pencil
- picture sources

What jobs did people do in the Middle Ages?

You are going to examine a number of pictures from the Middle Ages. They will give you clues about what people did. They might show the King ruling over his country. They might show an old woman helping to make bread.

Your task

Examine carefully each of the picture sources you have been given, and complete the table.

Picture Source	In this picture source there is/are...	I think his/her/their job was probably...
1	a man sitting on a throne. He is wearing a crown on his head. He is holding a sceptre.	king
1	two men with mitres and croziers (these look like sticks with crosses on the top).	bishop or archbishop
6	one man ploughing the field. Another man is whipping the oxen to make them move.	
7	_____ _____ _____	peasant
8	_____ _____ _____	peasant
9	_____ _____ _____	peasant
9	_____ _____ _____	reeve or bailiff

Picture Source	In this picture source there is/are...	I think his/her/their job was probably...
9	three men cutting the corn with scythes. They look very miserable.	peasant
10	a man standing on the horse's back. He is driving a cart which is loaded with hay.	
11	_____ _____ _____	miller
13	_____ _____ _____	peasant
14	a man standing behind the bellows making sure that the blacksmiths do their job properly.	
14	two men hammering at a piece of hot iron.	
15	a man carrying four loaves of bread to put in the oven.	
15	a woman breaking up branches to put on the fire.	helping the baker
15	_____ _____ _____	helping the butcher

☞

Picture Source	In this picture source there is/are...	I think his/her/their job was probably...
15	a man cutting the pig's throat	butcher
15	_____ _____ _____	helping the baker
16	an important-looking man drinking at a feast table.	
16	_____ _____ _____	servant
18	a woman sewing up a jacket and a man cutting some cloth.	dressmakers or tailors
18	_____ _____ _____	barber
20	some men building a large barn. They are using lathes, axes, saws and hammers.	
20	an important-looking man checking that all the builders are working.	architect

Resource Sheet

What jobs did people do in the Middle Ages?

These definitions can be copied to help the pupils describe the people's jobs.

lord

The lord was in charge of the village. Most people in the village worked for him.

bailiff and reeve

They were officials of the lord. They made sure that everyone farmed the lord's land properly.

villein

The villeins had no land of their own. They farmed the lord's land for him. He also let them farm some of his land for themselves.

craftsman

They made things for the other villagers, such as farm tools, or pots and pans. They usually worked on the land as well.

freeman

The freemen rented land from the lord. They also had to do work for the lord. They were better off than the villeins.

merchant

Merchants travelled around the country selling things like wool and cloth.

steward

He was an 'official of the lord'. He made sure that everybody paid their rent.

32

You will need
- pen or pencil
- picture sources

The Peasants' Year

The calendar below shows you the kinds of jobs that men and women in the village had to do through the year.

Your task

Look through all the picture sources you have been given. Which times of year do they show?

● ●

All year round

Firewood had to be collected, drainage ditches dug, the animals had to be looked after and the peasants' houses had to be repaired.

January

Much time was spent on work around the house – getting firewood and turfs, planting vegetables in the garden.

February

Ploughing began. Women or children helped to drive the oxen. The soil was sometimes prepared with manure.

March

The seed for the oats and barley had to be sown. A harrow was then used to cover the seeds over with soil. Other jobs included weeding and chasing birds away.

June

The sheep were sheared and the hay harvest in the meadow began. The hay was cut and then stacked in the barn. The cattle were allowed into the field to eat the stubble.

July

Hemp and flax were gathered in by the women, and laid out to dry ready for spinning.

August and September

This was harvest time. All the family helped. The men would scythe the crop until they had enough for a sheaf. The women tied up the sheaf. The sheaves had to be carted from the field. Both the scything and the carting were dangerous jobs. The carts had to be driven carefully or they would overturn.

The grain had to be separated from its stalk. This was called winnowing.

The lord provided food and drink and gave all the workers a feast when the harvest had been completed.

October

The field was sown with winter corn.

November

Some of the animals were butchered and the meat was salted and smoked so that it would keep through the winter.

Your task

Now complete this imaginary diary of a peasant's year. We have started each month off for you. You can write just a few words to complete each entry, or you can use your own research and write a few sentences.

January

It is very cold and wet. All we can do is

_____

February

It will soon be time to sow the seed again, so we have been getting the soil ready by

_____

March

I'm fed up with chasing away the birds. All week they have been trying to

_____

_____

April

It's been raining every day for weeks. We have been digging ditches to

_____

_____

May

All that rain last month made the house leak. Now the days are getting longer I've started doing some repairs. I have

_____

_____

June

Everyone is very busy. I've been

_____

July

The flax harvest was very good this year. We have _____

_____

August

The grain harvest was very good too. Everyone in the village came out to help. They _____

_____

September

The lord said he had never seen so much grain in his life. He laid on

_____

October

At least there's lots to eat at the moment with the harvest finished. But no sooner is one harvest done than I have to start

_____

November

The cottage is quieter since we

_____

_____

December

There was a big storm last night. Lots of trees were blown down. Everyone went out to _____

_____

33

There are three pages to this task

You will need

- pen or pencil
- picture sources
- crayons

How did people dress in the Middle Ages?

Your task

1. Choose two picture sources (from the Picture Pack or from your textbook) which show ordinary people in the Middle Ages. One picture should have a woman in it and one should have a man in it. You could choose Picture Sources 8 or 16.
2. Now complete the table below.

Picture Source _____   What the man is wearing
■ On his head he has a _____   ■ On his feet he is wearing _____   ■ He is also wearing _____   _____   _____   _____   ■ Draw one item of the man's clothing.   ■ Write here what you think the man's job was.   _____   _____   _____

ooo

☞

Picture Source _____ **What the woman is wearing**

■ On her head she has a _____

■ On her feet she is wearing _____

■ She is also wearing _____

_____

_____

_____

■ Draw one item of the woman's clothing.

■ Write here what you think the woman's job was.

_____

_____

_____

☞

What people wear nowadays

Your task

Now compare the clothes in the Middle Ages with the clothes today, and fill in the table below.

Drawing of a man wearing 1990s clothes whose job is

_____

Drawing of a woman wearing 1990s clothes whose job is

_____

The main differences are:

In medieval times	In modern times
■ Clothes were made from _____ _____	■ Clothes are made from _____ _____
■ Colours used were _____ _____	■ Colours used are _____ _____
■ The men wore _____ _____	■ The men wear _____ _____
■ The women wore _____ _____	■ The women wear _____ _____

34

You will need

- pen or pencil
- picture sources
- crayons

What did people eat in the Middle Ages?

Your task

1. Look through all the picture sources in the Picture Pack and select up to four pictures which you think might help you answer the question 'What did people eat in the Middle Ages?'. They might show people cutting wheat to make bread. They might show drawings of fruit around the border of the picture. You might find blackbirds or pigeons flying, or animals being killed. If you want help in choosing pictures, talk to your teacher.

2. Examine each of your pictures very carefully and use it to complete this table. An example has been done for you.

Picture Source	This makes me think people in the Middle Ages ate...	The evidence in the picture is...
9	horse meat	There are three horses in the picture. When a horse died people would not just throw away the meat. They would eat it.

☞

Written sources about food

Written sources as well as picture sources can help us find out about what people ate in the Middle Ages.

Your task

Here are four written sources. Use them to fill in the table on the next page.

SOURCE 1 From the records of the village of Elton

Nine pence was paid by the Lord to a mason for mending the dairy.

SOURCE 2 From a medieval poem. The speaker is a poor peasant woman

I cannot afford to buy hens, or geese, or pigs. But I have two cheeses, some cream and some oatmeal cakes, and two bran loaves baked for my children; and I have parsley, herbs and plenty of cabbage.

SOURCE 3 From the records of the daily expenses of Eleanor, Countess of Leicester, in 1265. Her husband was the most important baron in the country

Much white bread was eaten.

■ *Large amounts of meat and fish were bought. The meat included oxen, pork, sheep and geese.*

■ *'Stockfish' were popular. These were cod without their heads, gutted and dried in the sun. Other fish included 32 eels, a porpoise and a whale.*

■ *Much beer and wine was drunk. Much of the beer was flavoured with spices.*

■ *Many eggs were used.*

■ *Fish was often salted or smoked, baked or made into pies. Meat was preferred fried.*

■ *All foods were heavily spiced.*

SOURCE 4 A medieval recipe for a rich household

Make a broth by simmering calves' feet and shins in white wine until they are soft. Strain the broth and pour it over pork ribs and young chickens.

Simmer until the meat is firm. Skim off the fat. Add pepper, saffron and vinegar. Allow to set and cover with almonds, a few curls of ginger and cloves.

Stuff the chicken with a mix of parsley, suet, mashed boiled egg yolks, pepper, cinnamon, saffron, a little pork and cloves.

☛ **What did people eat?**

Rich people ate...	Poor people ate...	Everyone ate...

Sir Geoffrey Luttrell's feast

Your task

Here is a picture of a rich gentleman, Sir Geoffrey Luttrell, and his family. They are eating a meal with two monks. However, the table is empty. Using the lists you have just made, draw all the foods that the family might have eaten on to the empty table. Label each plate of food. One example has been done for you.

It does not matter if you do not know how the food would be cooked and served. Just use your imagination.

a fish pie

34

Harvest feast in the village of Elton

Your task

Today the harvest has been completed in the village of Elton. The lord is providing a feast to celebrate. The villagers have put out a huge table in the barn. They have also brought some food of their own.

Using the chart you have already made, draw on the table some of the food that they might have eaten. Draw as many different foods as you can. Label each plate of food. One example has been done for you.

It does not matter if you do not know how the food would be cooked and served. Just use your imagination.

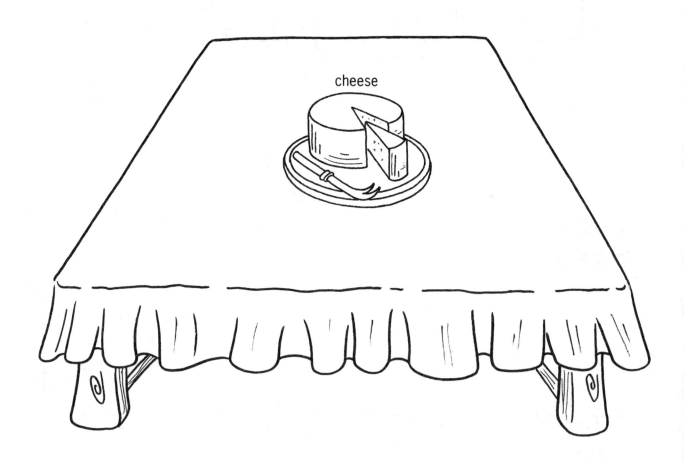

cheese

Food from the Middle Ages

cheese

eels

whitebait

stockfish

bread

oat cakes

shellfish gingerbread

spices

porpoise pudding

beer

wine

spiced pears

parsley

sage

rosemary

bay

boar's head

rose pudding

nuts

apples

apricots

broth

peacock pie

garlic

goose pie

grapes

cherries

plums

figs

meatballs

spinach

peas

radishes

lettuce

leek

Not a medieval village

Ernest Muddle has drawn a picture of a medieval village, but he has included some things that do not belong in the Middle Ages. Now that you have found out a lot about life in a village in the Middle Ages, can you spot some of the things that are wrong in Ernest's picture?

Your task

Put a circle round every **anachronism** you can find. One example has been done for you.

You will need
- pen or pencil

♦ HISTORY DICTIONARY

The important words	My explanation of them
plague	_____
	_____

What was the 'Black Death' and what caused it?

The 'Black Death' is another name for the bubonic **plague**. The plague was a dreadful illness. People who caught it usually died within a week. First of all they would feel ill and hot all over. After that their bones and muscles would begin to ache. The worst bit was when they got huge round boils under their arms and in their groin. These boils were as big as apples or onions. They were full of poisonous pus.

These boils would get bigger and bigger. Then a rash of black spots would appear on people's arms and body. By this time they would be screaming in agony. They would call for a drink of water but their throats and mouths would be too swollen to swallow it. Just before they died, the boils under their arms would explode. Out of the boils would come the most horrible-smelling black pus anyone had ever seen.

Some people tried to stick needles into the boils as soon as they appeared. But this didn't work. Some doctors gave people drinks of mercury, which is poisonous, or tried to burn the boils off their patients' bodies. Some people tried to rub soothing ointments and herbs into the boils. Nothing seemed to work.

☞

The spread of the Black Death

There were regular outbreaks of plague throughout the Middle Ages. The reason why everyone remembers the Black Death of 1348 more than any other plague, was because so many people died from it. In just a few months the population was nearly halved. There were 3 million people in England at that time. This means that nearly 1.5 million people died. Whole villages were wiped out.

You can easily imagine that people were very, very frightened of the Black Death.

On page 3 there is a timeline of the spread of the Black Death. It shows you when the disease first began. It explains **where** it spread, and some of the descriptions tell you **how** people thought it spread.

Your task

1. Look at the map of Europe and Asia on page 4. Some of the places named in the timeline are shown on the map. In the box next to each place write in the **date** when the Black Death arrived there. (You can get this information from the timeline.)

2. Draw a dotted line like this ....< .....< .....< to show the plague spreading from place to place.

3. Write '**plague starts**' and '**plague reaches England**' in the correct places on your map.

4. Did the plague move on anywhere else after it had reached England?

_____

5. Write a paragraph on the spread of the plague.

_____

_____

_____

_____

_____

_____

Discuss these questions with your teacher.
1. **How did the people of Strasbourg react to the plague?**
2. **Why do you think they acted like this?**

☞

Timeline showing the spread of the Black Death across Asia and Europe

Date	Description of how the plague spread
1345	In China and India there was a huge fire. It came down from heaven and killed all the people and animals. The winds from this fire blew across the land, killing many people.
1347	Twelve ships sailed into the harbour of Messina in Sicily. The sailors were all dying of a dreadful disease.
1348	The plague reached the city of Florence in Italy. Everyone thought it was because God was angry about people's bad behaviour. They tried to clean the streets and stop sick people coming into the city but nothing could stop the disease.
1348	In June two ships sailed into Melcombe in Dorset. A sailor on one of the ships had the plague. He had caught the disease in France. He spread the plague amongst the people who lived in Melcombe. They were the first people in England to get it.
1349	The Lord Mayor of London ordered people to remove all the human dung and filth from the streets. He said that this filth was infecting the air and making it poisonous.
1349	Some people in Germany began whipping themselves. They thought that God had sent the plague to punish them for their sins.
1349	Jews were burned in Strasbourg. This was because people thought that they had put poison in the water.

Map showing the spread of the Black Death across Asia and Europe

Use the timeline to show when the plague reached each place named on the map.

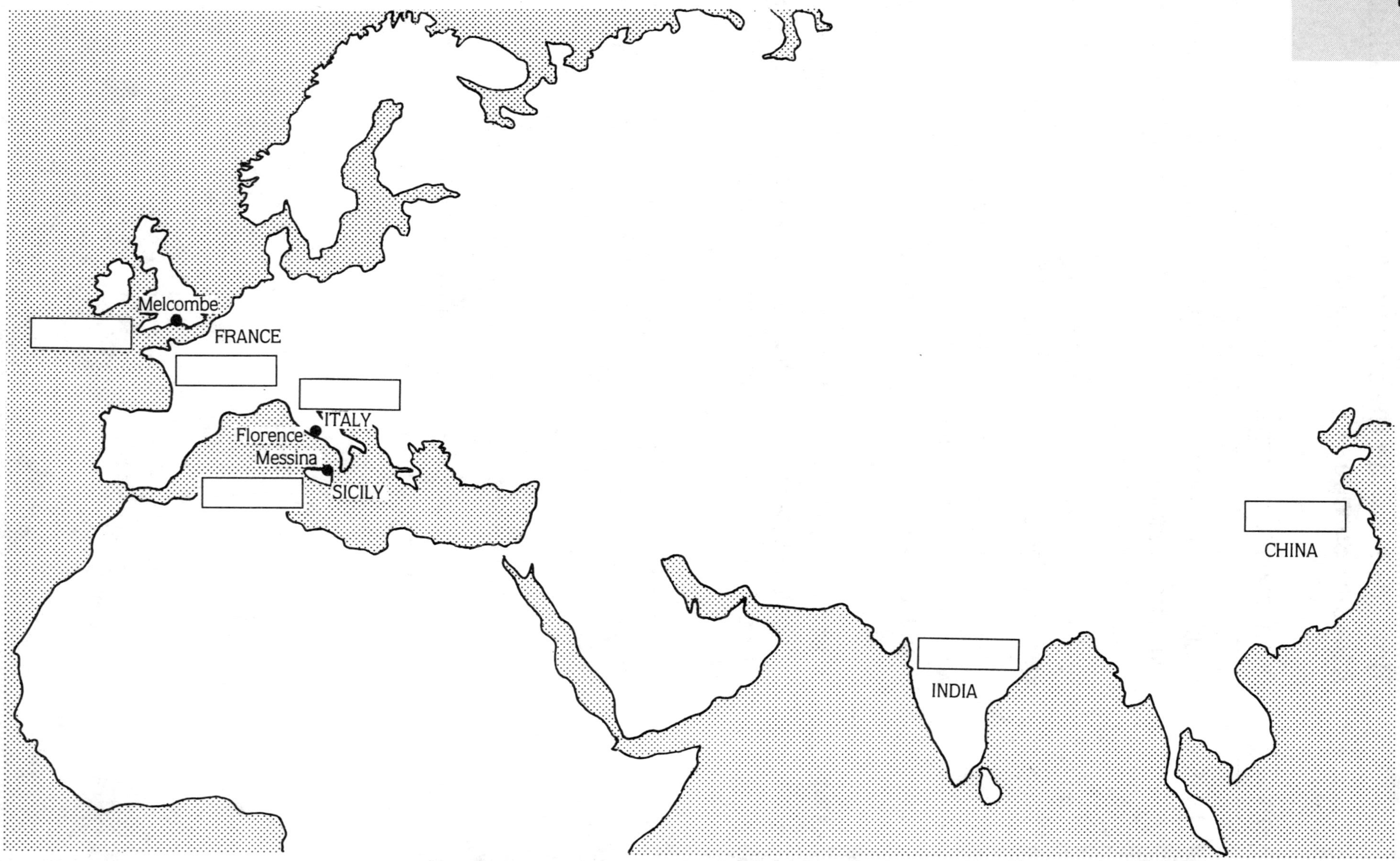

CHINA

INDIA

FRANCE

Melcombe

ITALY

Florence

Messina

SICILY

MEDIEVAL REALMS SUPPORT MATERIALS

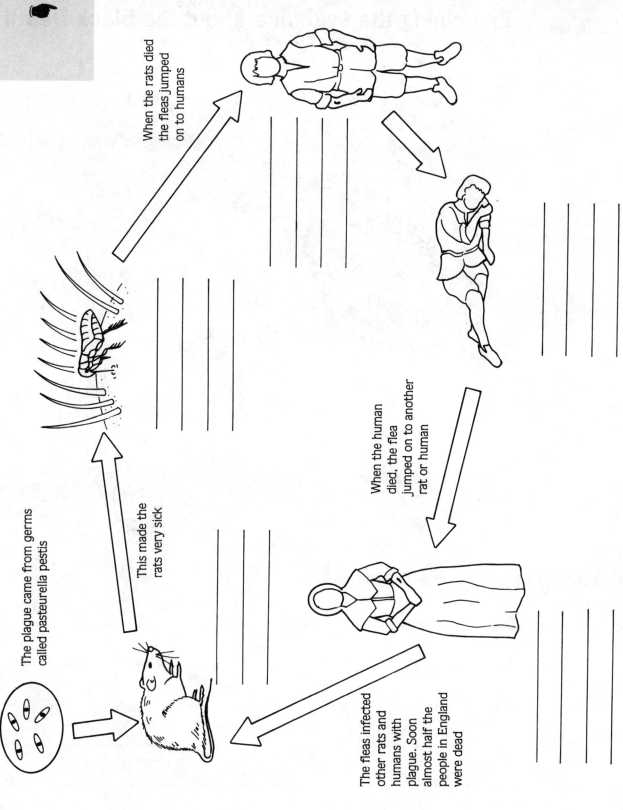

When the rats died the fleas jumped on to humans

When the human died, the flea jumped on to another rat or human

This made the rats very sick

The plague came from germs called pasteurella pestis

The fleas infected other rats and humans with plague. Soon almost half the people in England were dead

How bubonic plague was caught by humans

Your task

This diagram shows how bubonic plague spread.

Complete it by adding the following labels:

The fleas bit the humans

The humans died

Fleas sucked the rats' blood

The plague germs lived in rats' blood

The flea bit another human

MEDIEVAL REALMS SUPPORT MATERIALS

37

Examining the evidence about the Black Death

You will need

- pen or pencil
- Picture Source 21

Your task

Look at this drawing very carefully. It is copied from Picture Source 21.

1. Describe what is happening in the picture.

_____

_____

_____

_____

_____

2. Why do you think the horse and its rider are skeletons?

_____

_____

_____

☞

3. Now look at the whole picture (Picture Source 21). Which of these words or phrases would you use to describe it? Underline them in pencil.

■ sad   ■ bright   ■ happy

■ gloomy   ■ frightening   ■ ghostly

■ cheerful   ■ makes you think you ■ funny
                       are going to die
■ full of fear   ■ exaggerated

4. How did the artist try to scare people who looked at the picture?

_____

_____

_____

_____

5. Read Source 1 and then in the space below write your explanation of why people called the bubonic plague the 'Black Death'. You could underline the most important clue in Source 1 before you write your answer.

> **SOURCE 1** A medieval description of the plague
> *Lumps grow in the groin or armpit, some of which become as large as a common apple. Black spots appear on the arm or thigh.*

_____

_____

_____

_____

_____

_____

_____

38

You will need
- pen or pencil

Alice's Wedding Day

Alice lives in the village of Wharram Percy in Yorkshire. She is 25 years old and today is her wedding day. She is marrying Stephen, who drives packhorses for a wool merchant.

Your task

1. Read the story carefully.
2. Read it a second time, and this time underline:
a) the name of the place where Stephen lives
b) the things he brought with him to Wharram Percy.

Story

Alice woke up to the sound of church bells ringing. It was a beautiful sunny morning, and a perfect day for a wedding. Alice was marrying Stephen. He drove packhorses for a wool merchant who lived in Southampton.

They had met four months ago, on a chilly April day. Stephen had stopped at Wharram Percy on his way to York. He had some fine materials to sell and Alice had chosen some bright, scarlet ribbon. Alice could still remember the way he had smiled at her. Alice had smiled back.

A week later, Stephen had called again, on his way back from York. This time he stayed a whole month.

If you like that ribbon you can have it for nothing.

Alice met Stephen when he and his packhorses stopped in Wharram Percy on their way to York

At the end of the month Stephen asked Alice to marry him. It was hard for Alice to decide. He wanted her to live far away in Southampton. It was a long way to travel.

'You must go,' said Alice's mother. 'Stephen is a good man. He will take care of you.' So Alice agreed to marry him. The wedding day was set for the 15th of August.

Stephen went off back to Southampton, driving his packhorses. He had promised to find a nice place for them to live, and he said he'd be back in good time for the wedding.

'I will bring you a fine wedding dress too!' he added with a smile, as he rode away.

☞

And now the wedding was only a few hours away. Alice was so excited. She thought back to last night when Stephen had arrived.

How lovely it had been to see him again. He had arrived long after sunset. Alice was waiting with her parents and her best friend Sarah. Almost everyone else in the village was asleep.

Stephen arrived from Southampton. He said people there were dying from a dreadful sickness

Stephen was cold, tired and hungry. He had been travelling for two whole weeks. And he was full of stories of a strange and terrible sickness that he had left behind in Southampton.

Alice said to Sarah, 'He is so tired he is talking nonsense!'

'People in Southampton are dying of boils that are as large as onions,' Stephen said. 'When the boils burst, the smell is so bad that even the dogs and rats die of fright. No amount of water can stop people's thirst.'

Her parents laughed at this.

Alice's father said, 'There must be a great many Jews in Southampton who poison the air with their evil ways!'

Stephen got cross because people were teasing him.

Things got better once Stephen had eaten the hunk of cheese and drunk the warm broth that Alice had prepared for him. He went out to his packhorse and carried a

huge bag into the house. Inside the bag was the most beautiful dress Alice had ever seen. It was cream and gold with scarlet embroidery to match the ribbons Alice had chosen all those months ago. It was Stephen's wedding present to her!

Alice shook the dress out. Some fleas jumped out and made her father swear as they bit him. But the dress was perfect. Alice giggled as her friend Sarah tried it on first. Then her mother wanted

Stephen had brought a wedding dress for Alice. There were fleas in it but she soon shook them out

to try it too. Alice could not stop laughing at her mother trying to squeeze into her wedding dress.

'You'll frighten all the fleas away and squash the ones that dare stay!' her father said.

Stephen had brought other things for the wedding feast too. There was a 'side' of ham, some cheese wrapped in muslin cloth and, to Alice's great delight, some salt, cinnamon, nutmeg and pepper. 'Stephen must have some rich friends in Southampton to be able to get these spices,' thought Alice.

Stephen found a dead rat inside the bag which he had brought with him from Southampton

With a shudder Alice also remembered how Stephen had found a large black rat at the bottom of his bag. It was dead and Stephen had thrown it on the fire before Alice's mother could see it. Her mother hated rats. She said that rats were all right when they were alive, but that seeing a dead rat always brought bad luck on a family.

'But today there will be no bad luck,' Alice thought as she got out of bed. Today we will get married. The whole village will come to the feast. Then Stephen and I will set off for a new life in Southampton.'

Just then Alice's mother bustled in.

'Come on Alice, stop day-dreaming. We must fetch Stephen from cousin Elizabeth's house. The priest is expecting us at noon.'

Suddenly the door of the cottage was flung wide open. There stood Elizabeth. She looked very frightened.

'Whatever is the matter?' asked Alice.

Stephen was too ill to go to the wedding. He had a fever and a rash

'Go to my cottage quickly,' Elizabeth replied. 'Stephen is ill. He has a fever and keeps asking for you!'

Alice ran out of the house and across the path to Elizabeth's cottage. Stephen was still lying in bed. He groaned and lifted his head.

'Don't worry, Alice, it is only a chill,' he said. 'I must have caught it on my journey up from Southampton. I shall be better tomorrow. Go and tell the priest to wait till Monday. We can get married then.'

That evening Stephen got worse. He complained of terrible pains in his armpits and groin and a rash of black spots appeared on his arms and legs. What were they to do?

Alice was brave enough for all of them.

'Elizabeth,' she said, 'you must go and stay with Mother and Father. I will stay here with Stephen. Ask the wise woman for some sweet-smelling rosehip and feverfew to make tea. Leave all the food, herbs and drinks at the front door. I will come out to collect them. It will be better for everyone if only I touch Stephen from now on.'

With those words, Alice left her parents and cousin and went inside the cottage to look after Stephen.

Monday came and there was no wedding. Stephen was even worse.

For four days he lay groaning and crying on his bed. 'Don't touch me!' he would cry. 'God has sent his devils to punish me because I drank ale on Sundays. He is making me have this terrible thirst as a punishment!'

On the fifth day, Stephen turned his agonised face towards Alice.
'Pray to God that my soul reaches heaven. Call the priest! Call the priest! I am near to death! I must make my last confession.'

But it was already too late. Stephen's eyes rolled back into his head. His body shuddered and then all was still. Alice reached forward to pull the blanket over his face.

As she lifted it, the most dreadful stench hit her. Poor Stephen. Under his lifeless arms and in his groin were the largest boils Alice had ever seen. They had exploded and were oozing out a thick, slimy, black, foul-smelling pus. This was what caused the stench.

Stephen died and Alice found boils on his body

Alice burned everything that Stephen had touched

Alice was so brave. She lovingly wrapped Stephen's body in the blanket that he had been lying on. Then she went over to the bed where she had been sleeping, to collect another blanket. She wrapped Stephen's body in this too. Finally, Alice stoked up the fire in the middle of the room. Bit by bit she threw every scrap of clothing, the blanket, bedding, and food on to the fire. She added some sweet-smelling herbs, poked the fire once, then twice, looked at poor Stephen's shroud one more time and then slowly walked out of the cottage to tell her parents the bad news.

39

Bubonic or pneumonic plague?

Some historians think that the Black Death was actually two deadly plagues attacking at the same time with different causes and different effects.

Bubonic plague

This plague is carried by rats. Fleas bite the rats and become infected. The fleas then bite humans and pass the plague on to them.

Sufferers have a fever and large swellings in the groin and in the armpit. About 70 per cent of people who catch it die. It takes between four and seven days for them to die.

Pneumonic plague

This plague is caught through breathing. It attacks the lungs. Patients cough blood and spray out germs every time they breathe out.

The sufferer has a fever. Everyone who catches this plague dies after about two days.

Your task

Which plague do you think Stephen died from? Support your answer with evidence from the story 'Alice's Wedding Day'.

I think Stephen died of

_____

The evidence in the story which makes me think this is _____

_____

_____

_____

_____

40

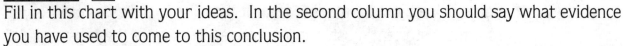

You will need

• pen or pencil

The Black Death in Wharram Percy

What do you think happened to all the people who lived in Wharram Percy?

Your task

Fill in this chart with your ideas. In the second column you should say what evidence you have used to come to this conclusion.

What happened?	The evidence
■ I think that Alice…	
■ I think that Alice's parents…	
■ I think that Alice's friend Sarah…	
■ I think that the rest of the village…	

41

There are three pages to this task

ooooooooooooooooooooooooooooooooooooooooooooooooooooooooooooooooo

Sources about the Black Death

You will need

- pen or pencil
- Tasks 36–38

In your study of the Black Death you have examined six different types of historical source. They were all interesting in their own way.

■ Some told you when the plague came to England.

■ Some told you why the plague came to England.

■ Some helped you to imagine what it was like to have the plague.

You, the historian, must decide which sources were the most helpful to you.

Your task

1. Look at the chart which starts below and put a circle round the description of each source you most agree with.

2. Give your reasons in the space provided.

3. Now complete the following sentence:

The historical source which was the most useful to me in finding out about the Black Death was

_____

_____

because _____

_____

_____

_____

_____

_____

_____

_____

Sources about the Black Death

For each source circle 'very useful', 'quite useful' or 'only helped a bit', and explain why you think this.

SOURCE 1

The background description of the Black Death (Task 36, page 1)

VERY USEFUL   QUITE USEFUL   ONLY HELPED A BIT

I think this because:

_____

_____

_____

SOURCE 2

The timeline showing how long it took for the plague to spread (Task 36, page 3)

VERY USEFUL   QUITE USEFUL   ONLY HELPED A BIT

I think this because:

_____

_____

_____

SOURCE 3

The map of Europe and Asia showing where the plague spread to (Task 36, page 4)

VERY USEFUL   QUITE USEFUL   ONLY HELPED A BIT

I think this because:

_____

_____

_____

SOURCE 4

The diagram showing how people caught the plague from fleas (Task 36, page 5)

VERY USEFUL   QUITE USEFUL   ONLY HELPED A BIT

I think this because:

_____

_____

SOURCE 5

The pictures and written evidence from medieval times (Task 37)

VERY USEFUL   QUITE USEFUL   ONLY HELPED A BIT

I think this because:

_____

_____

SOURCE 6

The imaginary story about Alice's wedding day (Task 38)

VERY USEFUL   QUITE USEFUL   ONLY HELPED A BIT

I think this because:

_____

_____

42

There are three pages to this task

∞∞∞∞∞∞∞∞∞∞∞∞∞∞∞∞∞∞∞∞∞∞∞∞∞∞∞∞∞∞∞

You will need
- crayons
- scissors
- glue

♦ **HISTORY DICTIONARY**

The important words	My explanation of them
tradesmen	_____
	_____
	_____
	_____
	_____
	_____

The growth of Ludlow

In 1066 there were very few towns in England. Almost everyone lived in villages. But one of the things that changed in England after William the Conqueror became king was that more towns appeared and more people began to live in towns.

Often these towns grew up around castles which had been built by Norman barons. To start with people lived inside the castle walls because the castle kept them safe from attack.

When there were too many people inside the castle wall, or when there was no longer any risk of being attacked, people began to build their houses outside the castle walls. Then they usually made new walls to protect their new houses and the castle became part of a town!

One town which grew up in this way was Ludlow in Shropshire. You are going to find out what Ludlow was like in the Middle Ages.

Your task

1. Look at the map of Ludlow on page 2. Shade in these main features:
   ■ the river (blue)
   ■ the roads (red)
   ■ the castle and the church (brown)
   ■ the areas outside the town wall (green).
2. Cut out the descriptions of Ludlow on page 3.
3. Match each one with a box on the map on page 2. The first one has been done for you.
4. When you are sure you have the descriptions in the right boxes, stick them in place.

Map of Ludlow

Put the descriptions in the right boxes. The first one has been done for you.

A
Ludlow was built near a good place to cross the river Teme.

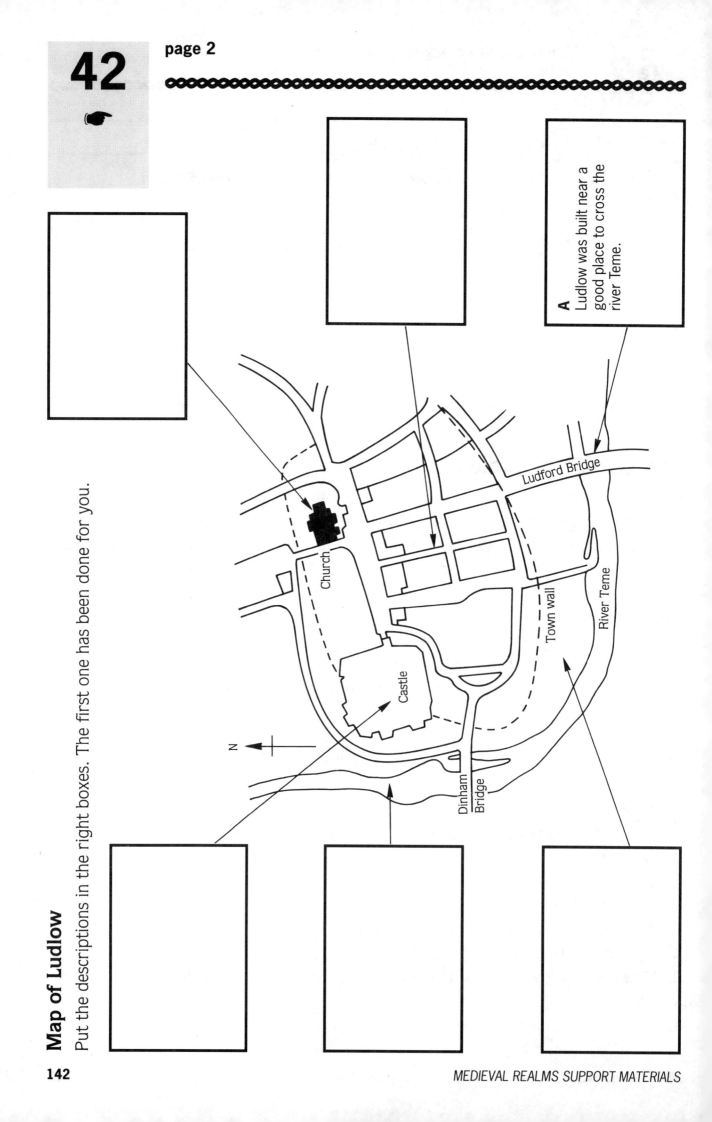

Church

Ludford Bridge

Town wall

River Teme

Castle

N

Dinham Bridge

42

Descriptions of Ludlow in the Middle Ages

Cut out these descriptions and match them with the boxes on the map.

A
Ludlow was built near a good place to cross the river Teme.

B
Ludlow's neat street pattern was planned from the start. There was a broad High Street (where markets were held) with side roads coming off it.

C
As the town became richer, a grand church was built.

D
The river Teme runs through a gorge to the west of the town. This swift-flowing river ran the water mills for the town.

E
The **tradesmen** who lived in Ludlow still farmed the open fields outside the town.

F
Baron Roger began to build Ludlow Castle in 1086. The site for the castle was protected on three sides by high cliffs.

43

You will need
* pen or pencil

◆ **HISTORY DICTIONARY**

The important words	My explanation of them
pillory	_____
guild	_____

Trouble in Mill Street

You are going to read a story from the Middle Ages.

James's parents run a bakery in Ludlow. In those days people did not have ovens at home, so they would make their bread dough at home, and then take it to the baker's to be baked.

In this story James and his dog Growler come to the rescue when things are going badly for James's parents.

Your task

1. Read this story carefully, and find out exactly what happens to James and his dog.
2. When you have finished reading the story you will try to match the events in the story with a written source about a medieval crime.

Story

James walked into the front room of his parents' bakery. The room was dark, even though there was daylight outside.

'How strange,' he thought. 'Why have the shutters been closed? Why is the bread still in the baskets? Why are the loaves not out on the stall for people to buy?'

James could hear his parents talking in the back room. His mother sounded upset and his father was shouting.

The people in the town say that we steal their dough.

James's parents were upset because no one would buy bread from their bakery

'What is wrong?' James asked as he entered the room.

'People have stopped bringing their dough to our bakery!' his mother cried. 'They say that the loaves are too small. And that we must be stealing some of their dough.

MEDIEVAL REALMS SUPPORT MATERIALS

☞ And they even refuse to buy our own loaves of bread. People say we put sawdust in them!'

'But that's not true, is it?' James asked.

'Of course it's not true. But what if they don't believe us? You know what will happen, don't you?' James's mother began to cry. 'They will stand us in the market place. With our heads and hands tied into a **pillory**. They'll throw rotten food at us. They'll hang dough around our necks.'

James looked anxiously at his father.

'Things are looking bad for us, James,' his father explained. 'All our customers have left us. They've started going to the old mill just past Dinham Bridge behind the castle. A new family of bakers has come to town. They run the mill and have set up a bakery too.'

'Are they allowed to do that?' asked James. 'There are three bakeries in Ludlow already.'

'If the **guild** masters allow them to set up here, then we must accept them,' said his father. 'But it's bad news for all of us.'

There's a queue outside the new bakery.

James decided to visit the new bakery

'But who is telling these lies about us?'

'I wish we knew, James.'

There was only one way to find out. James decided to visit the new bakery. But he wouldn't go alone, in case things got unpleasant. James whistled for his dog. Growler was a huge brown mongrel. He had sharp teeth and a loud bark. Growler was a very good guard dog. James would be safe with him.

The two of them set off up Mill Street towards the High Street. There were two other bakeries in Mill Street. The bakers were sitting outside their shops. There was no work to do. It was the same story for them as it was for James's parents. The same rumours. All their customers had gone to the new bakery as well.

It was a five-minute walk down past the castle. As James reached Dinham Bridge he saw a queue of people. It stretched all the way from the bridge down to the new bakery.

'What are you all waiting for?' James asked as he joined the queue.

☞

'We are waiting to visit the only honest baker in town,' said a plump lady. James recognised her. She had been one of his parents' most regular customers.

'But you always come to my father's bakery,' said James.

'Not since I heard about his dishonest practices,' the plump lady replied.

'My husband and I were in the ale house last night. Your parents' servant was telling everyone that the three bakers in Mill Street steal the dough that we bring them. Then they use it to bake loaves to sell at Stokesay Castle, ten miles down the road.'

A woman told James that his parents' servant had been spreading rumours about them in the ale house

James felt very angry. He knew that there were no servants in his family. James's mother did all the hard work.

'Don't lose your temper yet,' he said to himself. 'Wait till you see what is happening at the new bakery.'

The plump lady was still talking. 'Now this new baker has promised that if we bring our dough to his bakery every day, he'll give us one extra loaf a week for half a year. No one is going to turn down an offer like that, are they?'

As they were talking, the queue had wound itself round to the old mill and bakery. Soon it would be James's turn to buy his loaf of bread from the new people.

Just then, Growler began to snarl.

'Sshh Growler, or we'll never get to the bottom of this,' whispered James.

But Growler took no notice. Suddenly he bounded away from James and shot under the table where people were placing their dough to be baked. There was an agonised scream.

'Help, help! Get this wild animal off me. Help! It's bitten my leg!'

Everyone in the queue stared as out from underneath the table crawled a young man. He was covered in blood and dough.

The servant crawled out from under the dough table

☞

'Great heavens, it is the servant we talked to in the ale house,' cried the plump woman.

'So it is,' said a man further back in the queue.

A crowd began to gather around the unhappy servant. James seized his chance and crawled underneath the dough table to find out what the servant had been doing.

'You've certainly got some explaining to do,' said the plump woman to the servant and the baker. 'What's going on here... you didn't tell us you worked here.'

James crawled out from under the dough table. 'I can tell you what is going on. This baker is cheating you. Look at his dough table. It has holes in it. The servant has been pulling parts of your dough through the hole.'

The people in the queue were suddenly very angry. 'You mean he's been stealing our dough?' they shouted.

'Yes, and then the baker makes extra loaves from the stolen dough,' said James.

'I bet he sells the other loaves in other towns,' said another.

'And that free loaf once a week – well, it was made from our own dough all the time!' said the plump woman.

'They have made fools of us,' everyone shouted.

'Master James, we are so sorry,' said the plump woman. 'Will you run back to Mill Street and tell them their customers are coming back? Tell them to open up their shutters and get their ovens warm again.'

'My parents will report this to the guild master,' said James. 'He will put the baker and the servant in the pillories in the High Street.'

James and Growler raced back across the town to tell James's parents the good news. Very soon the old customers came back.

His mother and father were so happy to open their shop again that all their customers were given a free loaf of bread, 'just to remind them how foolish they were!' as his mother said, smiling.

The new baker and his servant were put in the pillory in the High Street

☞

Your task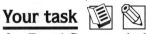

1. Read Source 1. Underline in red pen all the evidence in the source which matches the evidence in the story.

SOURCE 1 From London Court Records, 1327

John Bird the baker did cause a hole to be made upon a table in his bakehouse. And when his neighbours who 'baked' their bread at his oven came with their dough, John put the dough on the table. John had a servant sitting in secret beneath the table. The servant carefully opened the hole and bit by bit withdrew some of the dough.

  All those bakers beneath whose tables holes had been found should be put on the pillory, with dough hung from their necks, and those bakers whose tables did not have holes shall be put on the pillory, but without dough round their necks.

---

2. What is the main difference between the story of James and the story in Source 1?

_____

_____

_____

_____

_____

3. Why do you think the honest bakers in Source 1 were also put in the pillory?

_____

_____

_____

_____

_____

44

There are three pages to this task

You will need
- pen or pencil
- crayons

Shops and traders in Ludlow

In the Middle Ages streets in towns were often named after the type of shop or trader that could be found in that street.

Your task

1. What sort of shops or traders would you expect to find in these streets in Ludlow? You might be able to think of more than one. Write your answers in the space next to the names. The first one has been done for you.

Street name	Shops or traders selling...
■ Butchers' Row	*meat*
■ Mill Street	
■ Shoemakers' Row	
■ Lockiers' Row	
■ Fish Street	
■ Pepper Lane	
■ Drapers' Row	
■ Sheep Street	
■ Smith Street	

2. Look at the drawing on page 2. This shows a shoemaker's shop. List below the clues that prove this to you.

_____

_____

_____

3. Label the picture to explain what you think is happening at each of the numbered points.

4. On page 3 you can find some blank shop signs. Choose two shops from your list above and draw signs which tell people what was sold inside that shop. Remember that most people in the Middle Ages could not read.

44

☞

page 2

∞∞∞∞∞∞∞∞∞∞∞∞∞∞∞∞∞∞∞∞∞∞∞∞∞∞∞∞∞∞∞∞∞∞∞∞

A shoemaker's shop

Label the picture to explain what is happening at each of the numbered points.

☞

∞∞

Design a shop sign

Choose two Ludlow shops. Design a sign which shows what was sold inside each of the shops. Remember that most people in the Middle Ages could not read.

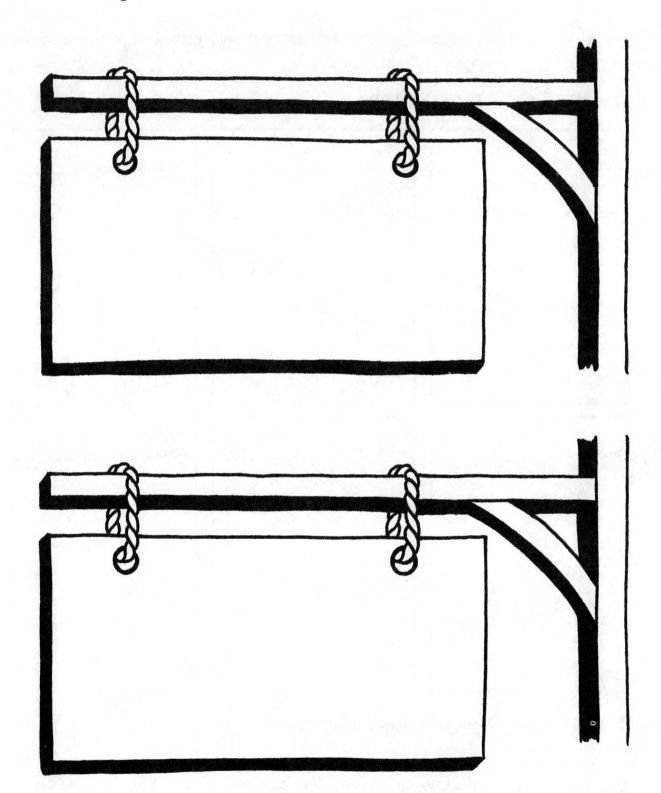

45

You will need
- pen or pencil

There are three pages to this task

Did people travel much in the Middle Ages?

Your task

Imagine you are going on a trip to Paris. Paris is the capital city of France.

1. In the boxes on this page list or draw a picture of all the different ways you could get there.

Travelling to Paris in the 1990s

We could ______________

____

We could ______________

____

We could ______________

____

We could ______________

____

We could ______________

____

We could ______________

____

2. Which of these is the fastest way to get to Paris?

____

3. Which of these is the slowest way to get to Paris?

____

☞

Your task

Now imagine you are a student who lived 600 years ago. You have been staying in England and are returning to your home in Paris.
In the boxes on this page write down or draw the different ways a student from 600 years ago would travel! Your teacher can give you ideas if you need help.

600 years ago people could _____

_____

600 years ago people could _____

_____

600 years ago people could _____

_____

How people travelled in the Middle Ages

SOURCE 1

Unloading grain from a barge. Drawn in the late fifteenth century

▶ SOURCE 2

Musicians. They travelled all over the country entertaining rich and poor people

SOURCE 3

One reason why people travelled was to go on pilgrimages to famous shrines such as Canterbury

45

☞

Your task ✎

1. Look at the ideas you have listed on pages 1 and 2. Which forms of transport were possible in the Middle Ages **and** in the 1990s?

_____

_____

_____

2. Which forms of transport are different?

_____

_____

3. What is the biggest difference between travelling to Paris nowadays and travelling to Paris in the Middle Ages?

_____

_____

_____

4. How does the way we travel nowadays make our lives different from the lives of people who lived in the Middle Ages?

_____

_____

_____

5. Do you think it was easy for people in the Middle Ages to travel a long way? Think carefully about this question.

_____

_____

_____

46

The Race to the King's Court

You will need
- one counter per player
- a dice
- good news/ bad news cards

Your task 1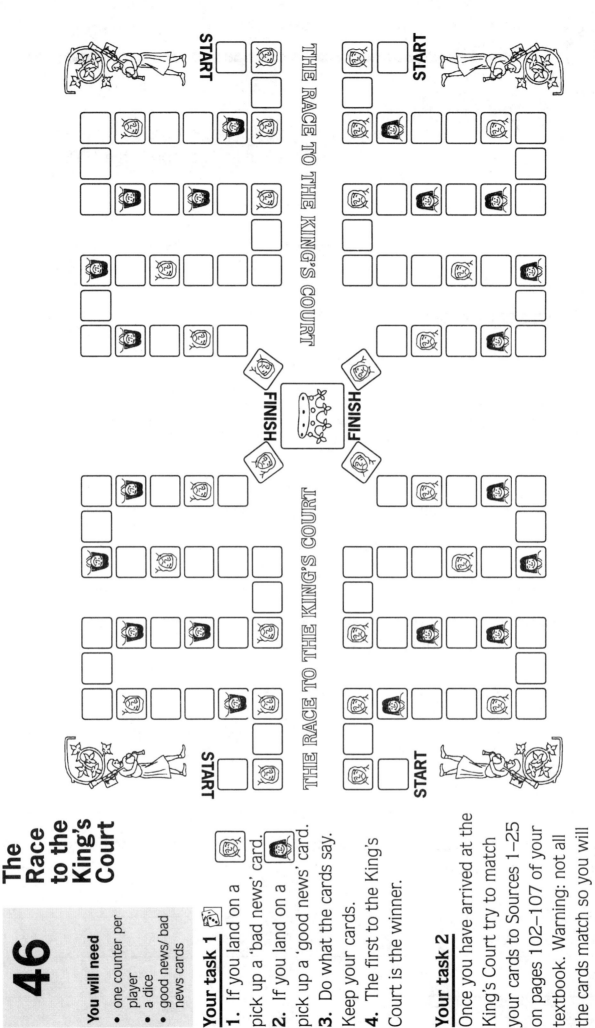

1. If you land on a pick up a 'bad news' card.
2. If you land on a pick up a 'good news' card.
3. Do what the cards say. Keep your cards.
4. The first to the King's Court is the winner.

Your task 2

Once you have arrived at the King's Court try to match your cards to Sources 1–25 on pages 102–107 of your textbook. Warning: not all the cards match so you will have to read and examine the sources very carefully.

Bad news cards

Copy these on to coloured paper or card, one set per game board.

BAD NEWS

A farmer has just
ploughed the road. You
cannot get across it. You
have to go through the
woods instead.

**Go back
one square**

BAD NEWS

You meet a man with
three packhorses. One of
them is lame. You help
him to carry their
woolpacks.

Miss a turn

BAD NEWS

As you walk along the
road, a harvest wagon
passes. A spike on the
wheel cuts your ankle. It
takes a long time to heal.

Miss two turns

BAD NEWS

You fall into a clay pit. It is
a huge hole dug by the
local miller. It is two days
before anyone finds you.

Miss a turn

BAD NEWS

Terrible floods and rain
have blocked the road.
You have to find another
route.

**Go back two
squares**

BAD NEWS

You see a gang of men
with swords and helmets.
They are attacking an old
man. You run and hide in
the woods.

**Go back one
square**

Bad news cards

Copy these on to coloured paper or card, one set per game board.

BAD NEWS

You come to a bridge across the river. It is broken. You have to walk six miles to the next bridge.

Go back one square

BAD NEWS

You stop to help some men unload grain from a barge. They think you want to steal it! They chase you away.

Go back one square

BAD NEWS

You meet a group of travellers going to a fair. They persuade you to go there with them.

Go back three squares

BAD NEWS

You want to cross a river but the ferry is not working. The ferryman has broken an oar. You help him to mend it.

Miss a turn

BAD NEWS

You meet a friendly shoemaker from Stratford. You drink some ale. You fall asleep.

Miss a turn

BAD NEWS

You sleep by the road, and when you wake up the bag containing your musical pipes has disappeared. You spend five hours looking for it before you find it in a ditch.

Miss a turn

Good news cards

Copy these on to coloured paper or card, one set per game board. Use a different colour from the bad news cards.

GOOD NEWS

You come to a main road. It is in a very good state, so you can walk twice as quickly.

Have another turn

GOOD NEWS

You come to a river. You play a tune for the ferryman. He lets you have a place on his boat.

Move forward one square

GOOD NEWS

You come to a road where there are no bushes or ditches. This means you are safe from robbers.

Have another turn

GOOD NEWS

You are lost in the woods. Suddenly you see a knot. It is in the branches of a tree. It tells you that the main road is close by.

Move forward one square

GOOD NEWS

You reach a part of the road which has just been mended. This helps you to walk more quickly.

Move forward two squares

GOOD NEWS

You meet some people. They are going to visit the tomb of Saint Thomas Becket. They let you ride on their spare horse.

Move forward three squares

👉

Good news cards

Copy these on to coloured paper card one set per game board. Use a different colour from the bad news cards.

✂- - - - - - - - - - -

GOOD NEWS

You come to an ale house. You play a dance tune. The people like it and they give you a free meal. This makes you fit and strong.

Move forward one square

GOOD NEWS

You visit a village church. You light a candle to Saint Christopher. He is the saint who helps travellers.

Have another turn

GOOD NEWS

You meet some wool merchants who direct you to a quicker route than the one you are taking.

Have another turn

GOOD NEWS

You meet a kind lord and his family. You help him load his wagon with furniture. He lends you his horse.

Move forward two squares

GOOD NEWS

You find a new bridge over the river. This means you can cross safely.

Have another turn

GOOD NEWS

You come to a town with a market. You buy some new leggings and have your shoes mended. This helps you walk faster.

Move forward one square

47

You will need
- pen or pencil
- Picture Source 19
- crayons

♦ **HISTORY DICTIONARY**

The important words	My explanation of them
heaven	_____
	_____
hell	_____
	_____
	_____

Heaven and hell

The priest

During the Middle Ages, almost everyone in England went to church. At church the priest would teach the people about God and **heaven** and **hell**. This was why the Church was so important and so powerful. People went there to learn things from the priest. And whatever the priest said, they believed.

Heaven

On the walls of the church they saw pictures of God, angels, saints and devils.

The priest told them that God was good. He said that if people were good, they would go to heaven where God lived.

The priest told them that if they went to heaven they would live happily ever after with God and his angels.

Hell

The priest also told them that if they were bad, they would go to hell. This was where the Devil lived. The priest said that hell was a dreadful place, where wicked people were tortured and burnt for ever.

Look at Picture Source 19 from the Picture Pack. It is a painting found on the wall of a church. It shows a ladder going from Earth through hell and into heaven. The souls of dead men and women are trying to climb the ladder to get to heaven.

Your task 1

1. Get an outline drawing of the picture from your teacher.
2. Look for the murderers being put into a pot of boiling water. Colour them in green.
3. Look for a money lender burning on a fire. He is still counting his gold. Colour him in red.
4. Look for a bridge of spikes for dishonest tradesmen. Colour the tradesmen in brown.
5. Look for a woman having her hand bitten by a dog. Colour her in purple.
6. Look for a drunken man with a wine bottle. Colour him in blue.
7. Look for Jesus Christ defeating the Devil who has his hands tied. Label Jesus Christ and the Devil.
8. Find Saint Michael the Archangel who has a pair of scales in his hand. Label him.
9. Describe carefully in two or three sentences what you think Saint Michael is doing.

_____

_____

_____

_____

_____

_____

_____

_____

Your task 2

On page 3 there are some drawings of people from the Middle Ages.
They have seen the wall painting and are saying what they think about it. Read what they have to say and cross out the things people in the Middle Ages would probably not think.

Heaven and hell in the Middle Ages

Cross out the things that people in the Middle Ages would probably not think.

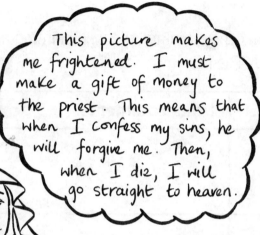

A — This picture makes me frightened. I must make a gift of money to the priest. This means that when I confess my sins, he will forgive me. Then, when I die, I will go straight to heaven.

D — This picture makes me laugh. I think that a madman painted it. Nobody believes in hell.

B — I keep looking at this picture. I don't want to die if it means I go to hell. I am terrified of hell. This picture gives me nightmares.

E — This picture makes me very scared. Supposing I go to hell when I die? I don't want to be burned and tortured. I will try to obey the priest all the time.

C — I don't believe that hell is like this. Anyway, I don't care. This is a silly picture. Nobody knows the real truth.

F — If this is what hell is like, I am going to obey the priest all the time. I will go to church every Sunday!

47

Your ideas about heaven and hell

Do people today still think the same things about heaven and hell as people in the Middle Ages did? Does the painting frighten *you*?

Your task

Ask people you know or your classmates what they think of the wall painting and if they agree with any of the people on page 3. Then fill in this table:

Name	Agrees with...	Other comments

48

You will need

- pen or pencil
- crayons

Who would go to heaven?

The three written sources in this task are stories which were told by priests in the Middle Ages.

Your task

1. Read each source carefully, and under each one write whether you think the person in the source would go to heaven or hell.
2. Explain why you think this.

SOURCE 1

There was once a woman who had hated another poor woman for more than seven years. When the woman went to church the priest told her to forgive her enemy. She said she had forgiven her.

After church, neighbours went to the woman's house. The woman said to them, 'Do you think I really forgave her with my heart as I did with my mouth? No!'

Then the devil came down and strangled her in front of everybody.

This person would go to _____

because she _____

_____

_____

_____

_____

_____

_____

SOURCE 2

A woman lived with a priest and they had four sons. After the priest died, the sons tried to persuade their mother to ask forgiveness for her deadly sin (because priests were not allowed to get married). But she refused.

The mother died soon after. For three nights the sons sat by her body. At midnight on the first night, to their terror, the coffin began to shake. Suddenly a devil appeared. It seized the body and dragged it towards the door. The sons tied the body to the coffin to keep it safe.

On the next night a whole group of devils invaded the house and took away the body to no one knows where!

This person would go to_____

because she_____

_____

_____

_____

_____

SOURCE 3

This priest knew the Bible, and preached from it faithfully.

He gave money to poor people from church money and from his own property.

He was happy with just a few possessions.

Whether it was raining or thundering, whether he was sick or sad he would visit everyone in his care.

This person would go to _____

because he _____

_____

_____

_____

_____

_____

_____

Your task

You are going to make your own wall painting. It has been started for you. Finish it off by showing what people in the Middle Ages would think happened to the three people described in Sources 1–3.

Remember, you should show what people in the Middle Ages would think, not what people today might think.

Remember too that you are trying to make the people in church afraid of doing evil things!

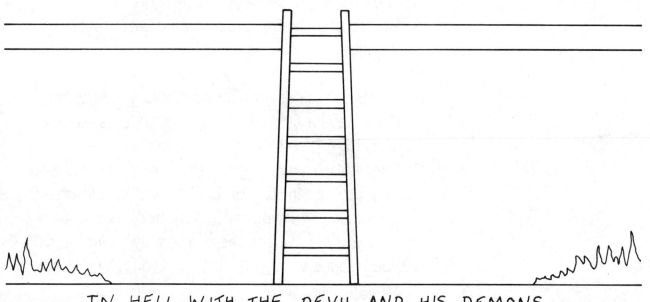

IN HEAVEN WITH GOD AND THE ANGELS

IN HELL WITH THE DEVIL AND HIS DEMONS

49

There are two pages to this task

You will need

- pen or pencil
- game board
- angel and devil cards
- dice and counters

◆ **HISTORY DICTIONARY**

The important words	My explanation of them
purgatory	_____
	_____

The Game of Heaven and Hell

In this game you are travelling through life and trying to get to heaven. Along the way there are devils' tails and angels' ladders.

Every time you go up a angel's ladder you get nearer heaven. Each time you go down a devil's tail you get nearer hell.

Will you get to heaven? Play the game and see.

Your task

1. If you land at the bottom of an angel's ladder,
a) move to the top of the ladder

b) pick up a , and

c) record on the score sheet on the next page what you did to get you nearer heaven.

2. If you land at the top of a devil's tail,
a) move to the bottom of the tail

b) pick up a , and

c) record on the score sheet on the next page what you did to send you towards hell.

3. At the end of the game count up how many angels and how many devils you have.

4. Record your fate at the bottom of your score sheet.

a) If you have all angels – well done! You go to heaven for ever.

b) If you have all devils – oh dear! You go to hell for ever.

c) If you have a mixture of angels and devils – don't despair! You go to **purgatory**, and wait…

5. Purgatory is a waiting place for people who are not going to be sent to hell, but may not yet deserve to go to heaven. If you are in purgatory, work out how long you must spend there. You may be lucky. If you've done enough good things you may still get straight to heaven.

a) Each devil gives you 10,000 years in purgatory

b) Each angel takes off 5,000 years in purgatory.

☞

The Game of Heaven and Hell: score sheet
Keep your score for each round.

✸ THE GAME OF HEAVEN AND HELL ✸

Your name _____

Square	What I did	My fate Angel	Devil
(Example) 37	I threw stones on to my neighbour's land		1
	Totals		

My fate

I go to _____ for _____

The Game of Heaven and Hell

Make one enlarged photocopy of the game board for each group playing the game.

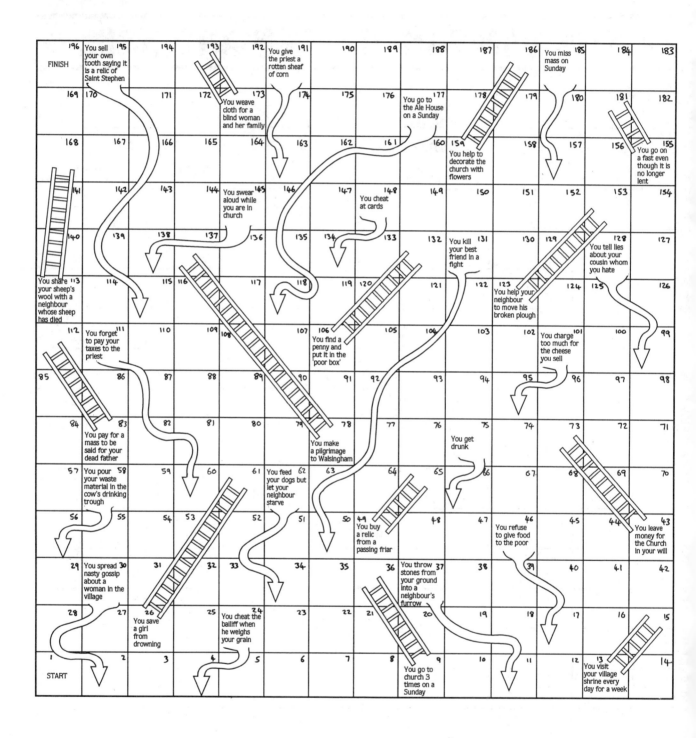

Angel cards for the Game of Heaven and Hell

Copy on to white card, one sheet per player. Cut out to make a pile.

a heavenly angel

a heavenly angel

a heavenly angel

a heavenly angel

a heavenly angel

a heavenly angel

Devil cards for the Game of Heaven and Hell

Copy on to red card, one sheet per player. Cut out to make a pile.

a hellish devil

a hellish devil

a hellish devil

a hellish devil

a hellish devil

a hellish devil

50

There are four pages to this task

You will need
- pen or pencil
- glue
- scissors

♦ **HISTORY DICTIONARY**

The important words	My explanation of them
archbishop	_____
	_____
	_____
the Church	_____
	_____
	_____
the Pope	_____
	_____
	_____
priest	_____
	_____
	_____
	_____

The murder of an archbishop

In the Middle Ages kings were very powerful. King Henry II was worried he was not powerful enough because he did not control the Church in England. Almost everyone in England went to church. The Church was ruled by the Pope who lived in Italy.

King Henry thought his friend Thomas Becket could help him, as the story on the next page shows. The story ends with a murder. See if you can work out what happened and why.

Your task

1. Cut out the five pictures on page 2, and the five explanations on page 3.
2. Match each picture with an explanation.
3. Put them in the proper order. Put the first part of the story on your left. Add the rest of the story so that the end of the story is on your right.
4. Ask your teacher for a timeline. Glue the five pictures and explanations in the right place on your timeline. Leave the sixth box empty.

OO

The murder of an archbishop: pictures

Cut out these pictures and match them with the explanations.

1162

1162

1163

1170

1170

1170

The murder of an archbishop: explanations

Cut out these explanations and match them with the pictures.

✂

After six years Henry asked Thomas to come back to England. He hoped that Thomas would have changed his mind and would now do what he asked.

Thomas refused. Henry and Thomas argued again.

Thomas went back to Canterbury.

Henry told his soldiers about his arguments with Thomas Becket. The knights were very cross.

Henry asked, 'Who will get rid of this turbulent priest for me?' Some of the knights thought this meant that Henry wanted to kill Thomas.

Henry had a good friend called Thomas Becket. Henry thought Thomas could help him to control the Church.

'The priests obey the Pope, not me,' said Henry. 'The priests are very powerful. How can I run the country if they don't obey me? I want you to help me.'

Henry made Thomas Archbishop of Canterbury. This was the most important job in the Church in England. Only the Pope was more important.

Henry thought, 'Now that my friend is Archbishop, he will make his priests obey me instead of the Pope.'

Thomas did not do what Henry wanted. Thomas said, 'I'm the Archbishop now – you can't force me to to do what you want. The Pope is in charge of religion, not you. The priests will obey him, not you.'

Henry was very angry. He told Thomas to leave England. Thomas went to France for six years.

☜

The murder of an archbishop: what happened next?

You are going to use the two sources on this page to complete your story of Thomas Becket.

Your task 📖 ✏️

1. The picture below is an outline of Picture Source 22. Copy it into the empty box on your timeline.
2. Read Source 1.
3. In the empty box underneath your drawing now write your own explanation of what happened.

SOURCE 1 Written by Edward Grim, who saw Becket murdered

The murderers came with swords and axes.

They called out, 'Where is Thomas Becket, traitor to the King and the country?'

'You shall die this instant,' they cried.

He received a blow which separated the crown of his head, and scattered the brains and blood about the ground.

51

King Henry's reign

You will need
- pen or pencil

Here is another timeline for King Henry's reign. It has all the years on it from when Henry became King to when Archbishop Thomas was killed. Your other timeline went across the page. This timeline goes down the page.

Your task

1. Look at your explanations on page 3 of the last task and decide what the most important fact is in each.
2. Write these facts down in the right places on your timeline.

Date	Event
1154	Henry is crowned
1155	
1156	
1157	
1158	
1159	
1160	
1161	
1162	
1163	
1164	
1165	
1166	
1167	
1168	
1169	
1170	

52

You will need

- pen or pencil
- scissors
- glue
- Picture Source 22

The death of Thomas Becket

On the next page is an account of the murder of Thomas Becket by a man who saw it all happen.

Your task 1

1. Cut out the eight descriptions on page 2 and put them in the proper order.
2. When you are sure you have them in the correct order glue them on to a sheet of paper.

Your task 2

1. Underline any words and phrases in the descriptions which show that Becket was brave.
2. Do you think the person who wrote this account was on the side of Becket or the knights?

_____

_____

_____

3. Now look at Picture Source 22 from the Picture Pack. There are some things the picture can tell us, some things the written description can tell us, and some things both can tell us. Fill in the table below. Put a tick in the correct column to show which sources tell us about the following:

	Picture	Written source	Both
■ how the soldiers were dressed			
■ what everyone said			
■ what happened to Becket's head			
■ how many times Becket was hit			
■ how many knights there were			
■ what happened before the knights came into the church			

☞

The death of Thomas Becket

Cut out these descriptions and put them in the correct order.

✂

Then Becket lowered his head and put his hands together as if to pray.

The next blow separated the top of his head and his blood ran everywhere.

One of the five knights placed his foot on Becket's neck and scattered his brains about the floor.

The five murderers came with swords and axes. The monks cried out to Becket to flee to the church.

The monks pulled, dragged and pushed him into the church. The knights followed. Becket ordered the doors to be kept open.

They pulled and dragged him, trying to get him outside the church. But they could not move him.

One wicked knight suddenly leapt on him and struck him in the head with his sword. He received a second blow, but still he stood firm. At the third blow he fell on his knee, saying, 'For the name of Jesus I am ready to die'.

The knights called out, 'Where is Thomas Becket, traitor to the King and the country?' Becket was not afraid and came down the steps and answered, 'Here I am, no traitor to the King, but a priest.'
'You shall die this instant,' they cried.

53

The Murder of Thomas Becket: a play

Main characters
- ■ Narrator
- ■ Thomas Becket, Archbishop of Canterbury
- ■ King Henry II
- ■ First knight
- ■ Second knight
- ■ Third knight
- ■ Fourth knight
- ■ First monk
- ■ Second monk

SCENE 1. King Henry's Throne Room. Tower of London

Narrator   This is a play about two men who used to be friends.
One man, Henry, was the King of England.
The other man, Thomas, was the Archbishop of Canterbury.

(Henry steps forward to the table which has his crown, sceptre and orb on it)

King Henry   Hail good people. I am King of England.
Behold, my crown, my sceptre and my orb.

(He places the crown on his head and picks up the sceptre and orb)

King Henry   I have a good friend called Thomas.
He helps me to rule the country.
He makes sure that everyone pays taxes to me.
I think I will give him a reward.
He shall become Archbishop of Canterbury.
He should be able to help me win my battle with the Church.

(Henry calls to the first monk)

King Henry   Father Grim, go and fetch my friend Thomas.
First monk   Yes, your majesty. I think he is in the counting house.
Narrator   Father Grim set off to find Thomas whilst Henry went to fetch the
Archbishop's special mitre, crook and cross.

(Thomas arrives panting because he has had to run from the counting house. He bows to the King)

ooo

Thomas	Good day, your majesty, and how may I help you?
King Henry	My dear friend Thomas, I have some good news for you.
	Today you are to become Archbishop of Canterbury.
	You will be in charge of the Church in England.
	You will tell people to obey ME, not the Pope!
	Kneel down, Archbishop Thomas.
Narrator	So Thomas knelt down.
	Slowly King Henry put the mitre on Thomas' head.
	He put the cross around Thomas' neck.
	He put the shepherd's crook in his hand.

(Henry gives Thomas the mitre, cross and crook)

King Henry	Arise Thomas, Archbishop of Canterbury.

SCENE 2. King Henry's Throne Room. Tower of London

(King Henry and his knights are sitting on one side of the table. Thomas and his monks are on the other side)

Narrator	A few weeks later, Henry called Thomas to his throne room. He was very angry.
King Henry	I am very angry with you, Thomas.
	My knights tell me that you ask people to agree with the POPE, not me!

(He bangs his fist on the table)

	Is this true?
	Answer me.
Thomas	Yes, your majesty. It is true.
	But I only want them to agree with the Pope about religion.
	You are still the King.
	You are still in charge of the laws and taxes.
	You still own all the land.
First knight	This is not good enough, your majesty.
	He is a traitor!

(He stands up and swings his sword)

Second knight	He is a traitor, your majesty.
	He is not to be trusted.

Third knight	He is a thief and a liar.
	Do not let him fool you, your majesty.
Fourth knight	Our great Archbishop prefers a foreign Pope to his own King!
	Kill him, your majesty.

(They all begin swinging their swords)

King Henry	Oh, sit down all of you. Let us not be too hasty about this.
Narrator	King Henry was sad as well as angry.
	Thomas was his friend. Thomas had helped him for many years.
	Henry had a plan.
King Henry	Stand up, traitor Thomas and your two friends.
	You will be sent away to France.
	You will be banished for six years.
	Go now, before I change my mind.

(Thomas and the two monks hurry out of the room)

SCENE 3. King Henry's Throne Room. Tower of London

Narrator	The King was as good as his word.
	For six long years Archbishop Thomas Becket stayed in France.
	But King Henry missed him.
	The people of England missed him.
	Henry decided to invite Thomas back home.

(Henry and the four knights stride into the room)

King Henry	Well, good sirs. Do you think Archbishop Thomas will have come to his senses?
First knight	It is hard to say, your majesty. We must wait to hear him speak.
Second knight	Once a traitor, always a traitor. That's what I say!
Third knight	My spies tell me that Thomas is more friendly with the Pope than ever.
Fourth knight	A friend of the Pope is no friend to our King!
Narrator	Just then, Thomas came in with the two monks. He looked very tired and sad.
Thomas	Your majesty, I greet you. You look well.
	It does not seem six years since we last met.
King Henry	Well, six years it is and another sixty years it will be if you still support the Pope!

Thomas	I support you both, King Henry.
	The Pope is leader of the Church.
	You, the King, are leader of the country.
	That is all I have to say.
First monk	Your majesty, can't you leave him alone?

(pointing to Thomas)

You can see that he is very tired.

He has travelled a long way.

Second monk	The people of Canterbury want to see him.
	Let him go now.
	Thomas will do you no harm.
Narrator	The two monks took Archbishop Thomas by the shoulders and led him out of the room.
	The King lost his temper.
	He began to shout and stamp.
King Henry	How dare he say that!

(He bangs his fist on the table)

	How dare Thomas say that he supports both of us!
	I am more important than the Pope!
First knight	You are right, your majesty.
	The Pope is wicked.
	He collects taxes that belong to you.
Second knight	The Pope is a traitor to religion.
	Some people say that he eats live frogs!
Third knight	The Pope is a traitor.
	Archbishop Thomas is a traitor.
	Only YOU, the King, can be trusted.
Fourth knight	Thomas has gone too far this time.
Narrator	King Henry stood up.
	First he looked one way.
	Then he looked the other way.
	Then Henry roared…
King Henry	Who will get rid of this turbulent priest for me?
Knights together	Your wish is our command.

Narrator They rushed off into the night. King Henry sat down and put his head in his hands.

SCENE 4. Outside Canterbury Cathedral

Narrator Whilst all this was happening, Thomas and the two monks had reached Canterbury.
Thomas wanted to pray.
Suddenly there was a loud noise and a great deal of shouting.
It was the four knights.
They had followed Thomas all the way to Canterbury.

First monk Thomas, Thomas, come quickly.
Come with us into the cathedral.

Second monk The knights will not dare to hurt you once we are inside the church.

(The two monks drag Thomas into the cathedral)

Thomas Let the knights in. They will do no harm inside God's house.
Perhaps they will pray with me?

(Thomas kneels down at the altar)

Narrator Just then, the knights came crashing into the cathedral.
They shouted:

Knights together Where is Thomas Becket, traitor to his King and the country?

Thomas Here I am.
I am not a traitor to the King.
I am a priest.

Knights together You shall die this instant!

(The knights begin to drag him away from the altar. Thomas joins his hands in prayer)

First knight Die, traitor!

(He hits him over the head with his sword)

Second knight You asked for this, Thomas Becket.
May your brains rot and the worms eat them.
Death to the Archbishop!

(He too hits Thomas over the head with his sword)

●○

Thomas   For the sake of Our Lord Jesus Christ, I am ready to die.

(Falls on the ground)

Third and   The Archbishop is dead.
fourth knights Let us give his brains to the dogs of Canterbury.

(They cut Thomas' head in two [Pretend!])

Long live King Henry!

(Thomas lies dead and the knights stand over him in triumph)

Narrator   So the friendship ended in death.
King Henry was very sad.
He said that he had not wanted the knights to kill Thomas.
He said that it was all a big mistake.

First monk   Thomas our Archbishop is dead but his soul is in heaven.

Second monk   The people of England still love him.
The Pope loves him.
God loves him.
He will become a saint.

First monk   Thomas Becket was a great man.
He died for his beliefs.
He died for God.
Thomas was a martyr.

Second monk   In a thousand years' time, people will still remember him.

First monk   They will come and pray in our cathedral.
Let us pray together.

(Both monks kneel)

THE END

54

There are three pages to this task

∞∞∞∞∞∞∞∞∞∞∞∞∞∞∞∞∞∞∞∞∞∞∞∞∞∞∞∞∞∞∞∞∞∞∞∞

You will need
- pen or pencil

King John – an evil king?

Look at the outline drawing on the next page. It is from a painting of King John. He was King of England from 1199 to 1216. Some people say he was a bad king. Some people say he was a good king.

A good king?

The artist who painted this picture wanted to show that John was good.

Your task

1. Look at the picture carefully and complete these statements to show how the artist has made John look good.
   The artist has made King John look good and kind by showing him:

   ■ with a _____ face.

   ■ stroking _____

   ■ wearing a _____

   ■ sitting on a _____

   ■ surrounded by _____

2. The writing at the bottom of the picture is in Latin. It means

John King of England

   In the space below copy out the Latin words in the old-fashioned handwriting.

C&C pp. 134–35 *MEDIEVAL REALMS SUPPORT MATERIALS*

☞

King John

Find the things in this drawing which make King John look good or kind.

☛

A bad king?

Source 1 is a description of King John which was written by a monk who knew him. The monk did not like King John.

SOURCE 1

John captured Arthur (his young nephew). After he had kept him in prison for some time, John became drunk and possessed with the devil and murdered Arthur by his own hand. He tied a heavy stone to the body, and cast it into a river.

The monk says that King John:
- ■ put his nephew in prison
- ■ drank too much
- ■ had a devil inside him
- ■ murdered his nephew and threw his body in the river.

Your task

Look at the outline picture below. You have already seen this picture but some parts are now missing.

Imagine you are the monk who wrote the description of King John that you have just read. Add things to the picture to show that King John was bad.

55

You will need
- pen or pencil

◆ **HISTORY DICTIONARY**

The important words	My explanation of them
civil war	_____
	_____

What did John do when he was King?

Like most kings, John did some good things and some bad things.

On the next page is a set of cards. On each card is a sentence telling you about something which King John did.

Your task

1. Cut out the cards.
2. Sort the cards into two piles. One pile is for good things that King John did. The other pile is for bad things.
3. Now use the cards to fill in the table below.

Good things that King John did	Bad things that King John did

 Discuss these questions with your teacher:
1. In your opinion, what was the best thing that King John did and what was the worst thing that he did?
2. Do you think John would make a good king nowadays?

What did King John do?

Cut out these cards and sort them into good things and bad things.

✂

John won battles against Wales, Scotland and Ireland.	John made the rich barons pay a lot of tax.
John may have murdered his nephew.	John made England richer.
John made the navy (England's fighting ships) very strong.	John quarrelled with the Pope. So the Pope closed all the churches in England and no one could be married or buried.
John lost battles against France – and he lost land which had belonged to England.	John took land away from the monks and nuns.
John made sure that trials in law courts were fairer.	John fought a civil war with his barons.

56

You will need
- pen or pencil

♦ **HISTORY DICTIONARY**

The important words	My explanation of them
charter	_____
	_____
freemen	_____
	_____

Magna Carta – the Great Charter?

The Magna Carta was a list of demands written down by the barons in England.

There were only about 100 barons but they had large armies. They did not like what John was doing. They particularly hated all the new taxes he made them pay.

They fought a civil war against King John. They wrote down all the things they wanted John to do in the Magna Carta (the 'Great Charter').

The barons' demands included:

■ when a baron died, his son could have his land if he paid just £100 to the King

■ a baron would only have to pay tax if the bishops, earls and other barons agreed

■ **freemen** couldn't be put into prison without a trial.

Because the barons had such strong armies, King John had to agree to sign it.

Your task

1. Look at the picture on the next page and discuss it in class.
2. Complete the description on page 3 by studying the painting carefully.

These questions are to guide discussion of the picture on page 2. You can find a colour version of the picture as Source 1 on page 136 of *Contrasts and Connections* – although this line drawing is much more straightforward to interrogate.

John

1. Which person is King John?
2. Why has he got an unhappy expression on his face?
3. Which person is advising John to sign the Magna Carta?
4. Which person is threatening King John if he doesn't sign?

John's advisers

5. There are two other advisers standing to the right of King John (A and B). Why do you think one of them is standing between the sword blades and the King?

The barons

6. The man (C) who is threatening King John is a rich baron. His friends are in the picture too. How many other barons are there in the picture?
7. What do you think the barons would have done if King John hadn't signed the Magna Carta?

Teaching point

The Magna Carta only really helped the rich barons and the rich bishops. Everybody else in the country was ignored. The peasants who made up 90% of the population did not get a thing!

The churchmen

8. Find two monks and a bishop in the picture.
9. Describe what they are wearing.
10. Why do you think the monk and the bishop are whispering to each other?

The peasants

11. The royal flag above the platform has been struck by lightning. The cloth of the flag is on fire and is burning a poor peasant. Can you find him?
12. What message is the artist trying to give by showing a peasant being burned?
13. How many other peasants can you see?
14. How else does the artist try to show us that the peasants were badly treated?

The artist's intentions

15. Why do you think the artist painted the barons and the two advisers standing above King John in the picture?
16. Why have the storm clouds been painted lighter above King John's head than in other parts of the picture?
17. Why do you think there is no rain falling on King John when it is raining in other parts of the picture?

Overall

18. This painting is an **interpretation** of what really happened in 1215. How useful is it to you as historians?

56

☞

King John signs the Magna Carta

Complete this description of the picture on page 2.

This painting shows King John signing the Magna Carta.
It shows the following types of people:

- _____

- _____

- _____

- _____

    The barons got more than anyone else when King John signed the Magna Carta. The artist has made them look strong and bold by

_____

_____

_____

_____

    The churchmen got something from the Magna Carta. But they were worried that the barons were going to have too much power. The artist has shown this by

_____

_____

_____

_____

The peasants gained nothing at all from the Magna Carta. The artist has shown this by

_____

_____

_____

57

You will need
- pen or pencil
- crayons

♦ HISTORY DICTIONARY

The important words	My explanation of them
villeins	_____
	_____
revolt	_____
	_____

The Peasants' Revolt of 1381

In England, the ordinary people's lives were often very tough. All year round they worked hard as farmers or as craftsmen, yet they were poor, and sometimes they did not have enough food. Even so they still had to pay taxes to the lord of the manor.

One group of peasants – called the villeins – was particularly badly off. For example:
- they had to work for the lord without being paid
- they had to pay special extra taxes to the lord
- they could not leave their villages without the permission of their lord.

On the next page is the story of what happened when some of the peasants decided they had had enough, and joined a revolt. It is a true story, but there are different versions of what happened.

Your task

1. Read the story which starts below.
2. Find the map of South-East England on page 3, and in the boxes on the map write down what happened in each place during the Peasants' Revolt.

In Essex Thomas Brampton demanded that the people pay a new tax. The people said they would not pay any more. Thomas ordered them to be arrested. The people rose up and tried to kill him. Then they went from place to place to stir up other folk.

A tax collector was sent to Kent but the people rose up against him. They gathered at Canterbury. After cutting off the heads of three traitors they took 500 men from the town to London with them.

The story of the Peasants' Revolt

The leader of the people was an evil priest named John Ball. On their way to London they burned the manors of the Duke of Lancaster to the ground.

This made King Richard worried. He said that he would meet the peasants at Blackheath on the next day. But the King's advisers told him not to go. This made the peasants very angry.

The rebels from Kent and Essex met the King at Mile End near London. They asked that no men should be villeins. The King said they should all be free and pardoned them.

Wat Tyler went to the Tower of London with some men where they cut off the Archbishop's head and paraded it through the streets on wooden poles. That night they murdered 140 people and there were hideous cries all night.

57

Map of South-East England

In the boxes on the map write what happened in each place.

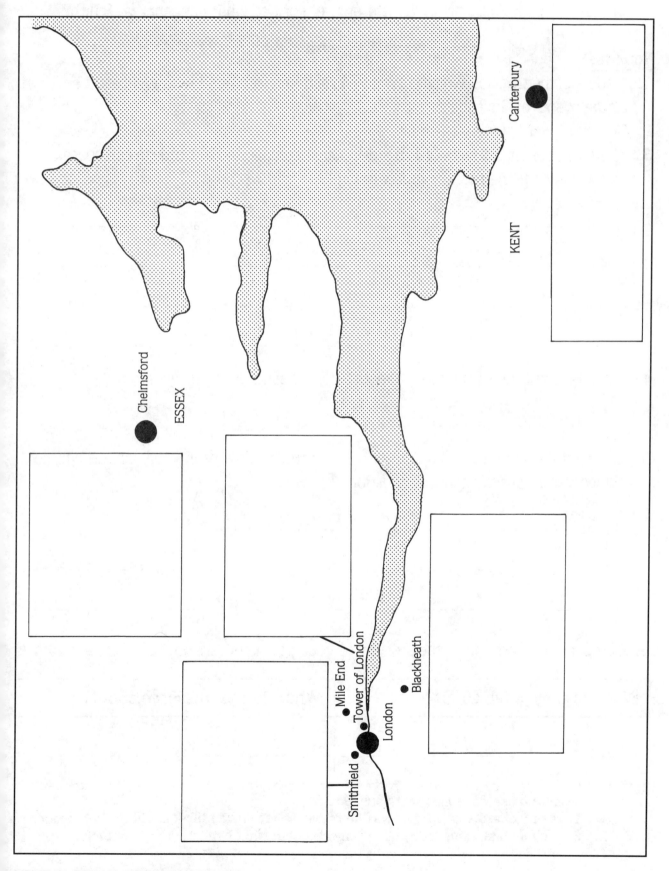

Canterbury

KENT

Chelmsford

ESSEX

Mile End

Tower of London

Blackheath

Smithfield

London

57

What happened next?

When the King found out what the peasants had done in London he agreed to meet them at Smithfield – just outside London's city wall.
On the next page there are two different versions of what happened at Smithfield.

Your task

1. Find a partner. Decide which of you will read Version A and who will read Version B of the events at Smithfield.
2. Read your version very carefully.
3. The most important facts of the story have been printed in **bold**. In the space below copy out the facts in your version.

_____

_____

_____

_____

4. Does your version of the story support the peasants or King Richard?

_____

5. In the space below copy out some of the words or phrases in your version which helped you to answer the last question.

_____

_____

_____

6. Compare your version of the story with your partner's version. Use a table like this:

What do they agree about?	What do they disagree about?

> **Discuss these questions with your teacher:**
> 1. Was Richard a coward or was he brave? What do you think about his behaviour?
> 2. Why do historians today still disagree about what happened at Smithfield?

Version A

PEASANTS BETRAYED!

London, 15 June 1381

Today King Richard proved what a coward and a trickster he is. Hiding behind bodyguards, Richard played his treacherous part in the bloody murder of peasant leader Wat Tyler. Tyler agreed to the meeting because he believed the King was going to help put right the evils which make life a misery for so many ordinary people. But Richard went back on all the promises he had made to help the people.

In good faith **Wat rode across to speak with the King, but was immediately surrounded by soldiers.** Out of sight of the peasants, **the** bloodthirsty **Mayor of London hacked down Tyler** as he spat out some of the drink he had been given. It is not clear whether the drink had been tampered with.

The King rode up to the peasants. He told them to follow him, and he would see that they got home safely, but **they soon found themselves surrounded by soldiers.**

Version B

BRAVE KING BEATS REBELS!

London, 15 June 1381

Today saw great celebrations after brave fourteen-year-old King Richard led his men to a brilliant victory over the peasant rebels who had brought death and destruction to the city.

With courage and majesty, **the King rode to Smithfield with his** trusted **followers to meet an army of** 20,000 angry **rebels.**

Tyler advanced to the King, dagger in hand and spat at him. **He then stabbed the Mayor of London in the stomach. The Mayor** bravely **struck** back **with his sword and Tyler fell to the ground,** screaming for revenge. **King Richard** calmly **strode forward to the peasants** and ordered them to obey him. Surprised, **they followed him to nearby fields,** where they surrendered. **The King let them go home safely.**

∞∞∞

You have already read two different accounts of the events at Smithfield. Here is a picture of the same events. This is an outline drawing of a picture painted in the Middle Ages. You can find a colour version in the Picture Pack (Picture Source 23).

Your task

Use the picture to complete your story strip of the Peasants' Revolt on page 2.

Draw your own pictures and write your own summary of what happened in the two empty boxes. In the first empty box show Wat Tyler being killed. In the second box show King Richard speaking to the peasants.

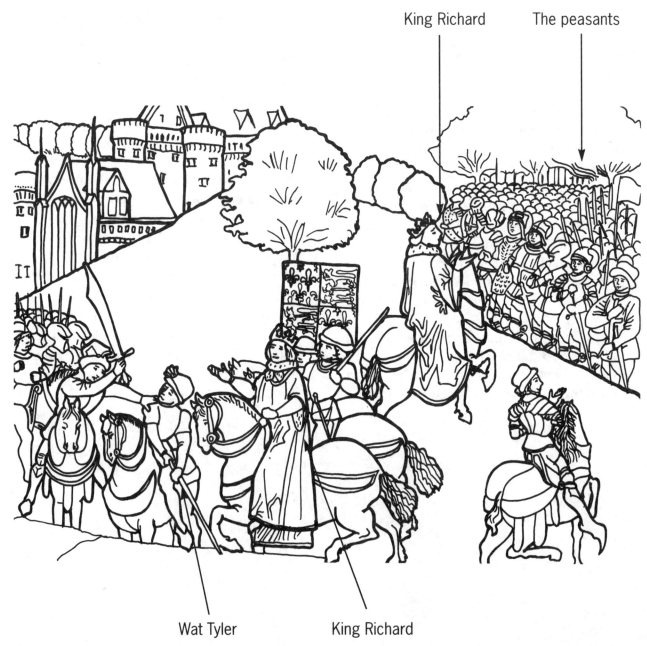

King Richard   The peasants

Wat Tyler   King Richard

58

You will need
- pen or pencil

Important events of the Middle Ages

Here is a timeline for the Middle Ages. Three important events have been put on it. But you probably think that there are other important events which should be included.

Your task

Choose three other events from the Middle Ages and mark them on the timeline in the right place.

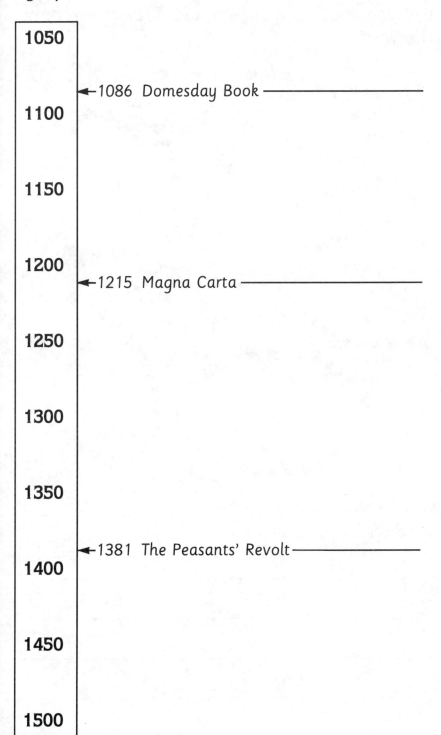

1050

◄—1086 Domesday Book ——————

1100

1150

1200

◄—1215 Magna Carta ——————

1250

1300

1350

◄—1381 The Peasants' Revolt——————

1400

1450

1500

59

You will need

• pen or pencil

What were the Middle Ages really like?

At the beginning of this course you looked at good and bad things about the Middle Ages. Now that you have become an expert in this period you will have seen that in some ways the Middle Ages were violent, but in other ways they were peaceful. Some people were clever and some people were cruel.

Your task 1

1. Look at the word stars on this page, and in each shape write or draw an event from the Middle Ages which fits that word.

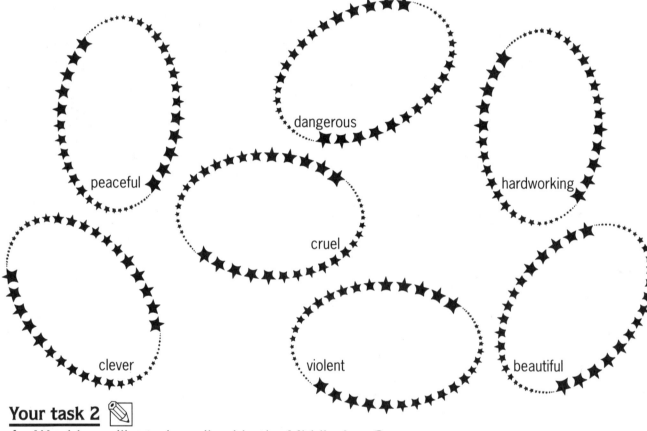

peaceful

dangerous

hardworking

cruel

clever

violent

beautiful

Your task 2

1. Would you like to have lived in the Middle Ages? _____

2. In the space below write five reasons for your answer.

_____

_____

_____

_____

_____

History Dictionary

Part 1: medieval people

archbishop

Archbishops were **priests** who had been put in charge of all the other priests and bishops in England. Archbishops had to obey the **King** and the **Pope**.

baron

Barons were sometimes called nobles or great **lords**. They were not as important as the **King**. Barons rented land from the King, paid taxes to him and had to obey him. Barons would provide **knights** and soldiers for the King's army when there was a war. Sometimes the King asked the barons for their advice.

bailiff

The bailiff worked for the **lord**. He made sure that everyone farmed the lord's land properly.

craftsman

A craftsman made things for the other villagers, such as farm tools, or pots and pans. Craftsmen usually worked on the land as well.

freeman

Freemen were **peasants** who had paid the **lord** money to be released from being **villeins**. They rented land from the lord. They also had to do work for the lord. They were usually better off than the villeins.

knight

Knights were soldiers who fought for the **King**. They paid taxes to the King. They rented land from the King.

the King

The King was in charge of the whole country. He was the ruler. Everyone had to obey him. The King could make all the laws. He decided when to go to war with another country. His eldest son became the next king.

lord (of the manor)

The lord was in charge of the village (which was also sometimes called a manor). Most people in the village worked for him.

merchant

Merchants lived mostly in towns. They bought and sold things to earn money. Merchants often travelled to other countries to sell their goods. Merchants had to obey the **King** and pay **taxes** to him.

peasant

Peasants lived in villages. They worked in the fields for the rich **barons** or **lords**. They had to obey the **King**. Peasants were very poor. They had to pay **taxes** to the King, the barons, and the Church. They had to give their best corn, bread, vegetables and beer to their lord. They had to fight in the King's armies when there was a war. Peasants were sometimes called serfs, **villeins**, cottars or **freemen**.

nun

Nuns were women who lived in a convent. They spent a lot of time praying to God in church. They tried to look after people who were poor or sick. Nuns had to obey the **King** and the **Pope**. They were not allowed to get married.

the Pope

The Pope was head of the Church. He was in charge of the **archbishops**. He lived in Rome.

priest

A priest ran each of the churches in England. There was a priest in almost every village. In church priests **baptised** (christened) babies, performed marriage services and held funerals. They had to obey the **King** and the **Pope**. Women could not be priests. Priests were not allowed to get married.

steward

The steward worked for the **lord of the manor**. He was more important than the **bailiff**. He made sure that everybody paid their rent.

reeve

The reeve worked for the **lord**. He made sure that everyone farmed the lord's land properly. He was chosen by the villagers.

villein

Villeins were **peasants** who had no land of their own. They farmed the **lord's** land for him. He also let them farm some of his land for themselves.

MEDIEVAL REALMS SUPPORT MATERIALS

Part 2: historical concepts and terms

anachronism
An anachronism is something which does not fit in a particular period of time.

archaeologist
An archaeologist is someone who studies objects or buildings which are left over from the past.

baptism
Baptism (also called christening) is when a baby is dipped in water in church and prayers are said for the baby by the **priest**. In the Middle Ages people believed you had to be baptised to go to heaven.

bias
Bias is when a **historical source** looks at an event from one person's point of view only and makes it clear which side it is on.

charter
A charter is a list of demands people give to their ruler.

chronological order
Chronological order is the order in which things happen. If you put events in chronological order you put the things which happened earlier before the things which happened later.

civil war
A civil war is when people from the same country fight against each other.

conqueror
The conqueror is the winner. William called himself 'the Conqueror' because he won the battle to become King of England.

The Domesday Book
The Domesday Book is the book in which William recorded everything that people in England owned.

evidence
Evidence is anything which we find out about the past. Historians look for evidence in **historical sources**.

feudal system
The feudal system was the system William used to keep people in England loyal to him. Under the feudal system the **peasants** had to work for the **lords**, and the lords for the **King**.

guild
A guild was a group of traders or **craftsmen**. The guild made rules for all its members to follow. A guild master ran the guild.

heaven
People in the Middle Ages believed that heaven was where God lived. All Christians tried to do what the **priests** told them so that they would go to heaven when they died.

hell
People in the Middle Ages believed that hell was where the Devil lived. All Christians feared that if they did not do what the **priests** told them, then they would be sent to hell when they died.

historical source
A historical source gives you **evidence** about the past. It can be a picture, a letter, a diary, an object – in fact anything left over from the past.

invasion
An invasion is when an army attacks and takes control of another country.

medieval
Medieval means 'from the Middle Ages'.

the Middle Ages
The Middle Ages is the name given to the period of British history from the **Norman** conquest of Britain in 1066 to the beginning of the Tudor period in 1485.

Norman
A Norman is someone from Normandy in North-west France – just over the sea from southern England.

pillory
The pillory looked like this:

It would be set up in the centre of a town or village and people who had done something wrong would be locked into it. People might throw things at them while they were locked in the pillory.

plague
The plague was a terrible disease which swept through England regularly during the Middle Ages. The worst plague was the Black Death in 1348 which killed almost half the people in England.

purgatory
People in the Middle Ages believed that purgatory was a place where most people were sent after they died. In purgatory they were punished for the things they had done wrong during their lives. The better Christian you had been, the less time you had to spend in purgatory. When you had been punished enough then you could go to **heaven**.

reconstruct
To reconstruct the past means to use **historical sources** to work out what life was like.

revolt
A revolt is a protest. In the Peasants' Revolt of 1381 the peasants protested against a new **tax** they were being forced to pay. Often a revolt can be very violent.

survey
In a survey people find out information about something. In the **Domesday** survey, the **King** sent people to find out what everyone in England owned, so that he could **tax** them on it.

tax
Tax was money people were forced to pay to the **King** or the Church.

timeline
A timeline is a line with dates on it. It can help you to remember in which order important things happened. It is useful in history because it gives us an overview of a period.

written sources
Written sources are **historical sources** which are written down, such as letters, diaries, stories and other records.

Black outlines of Picture Pack sources

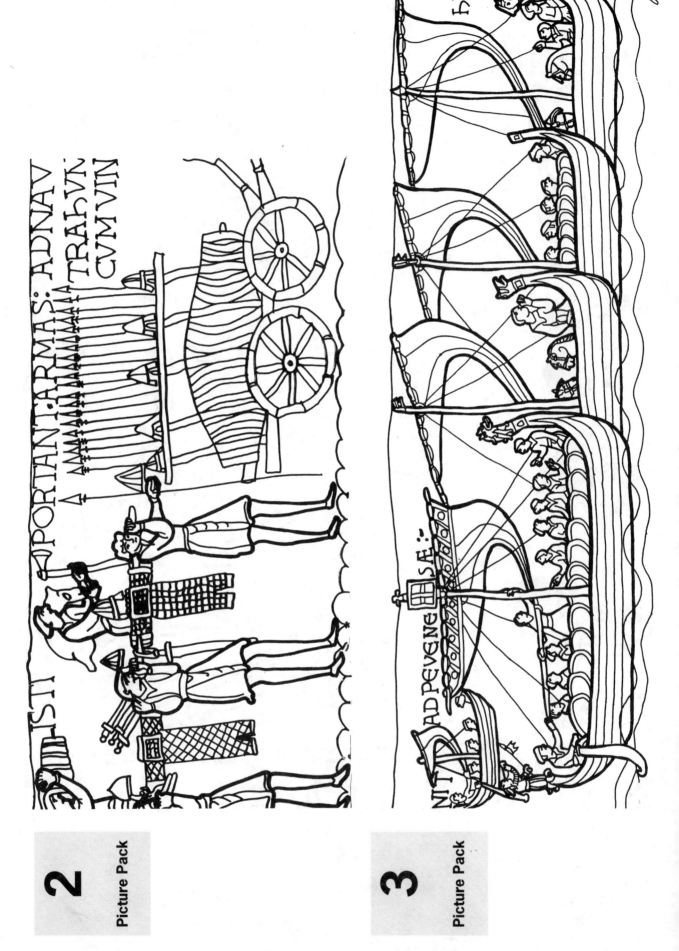

2

3

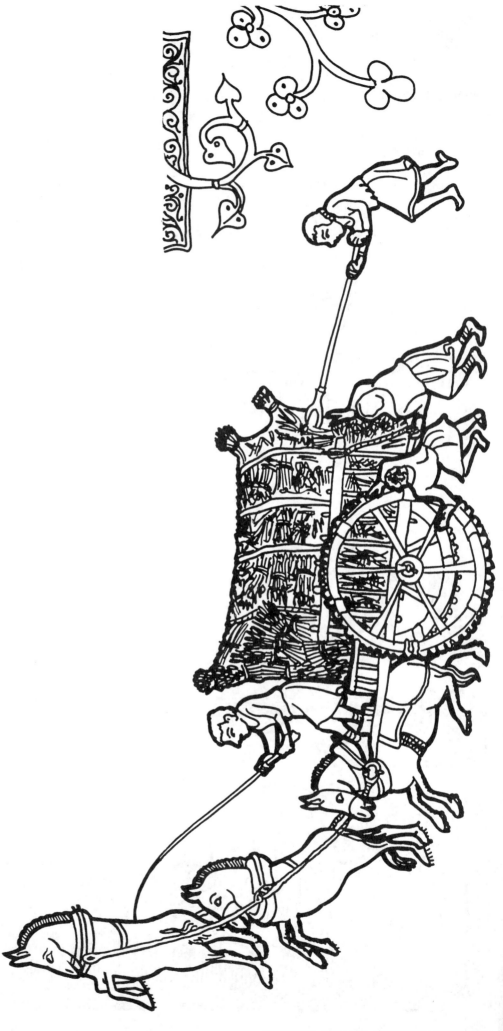

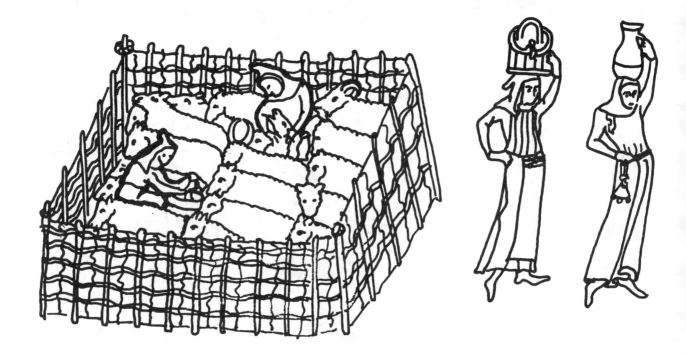

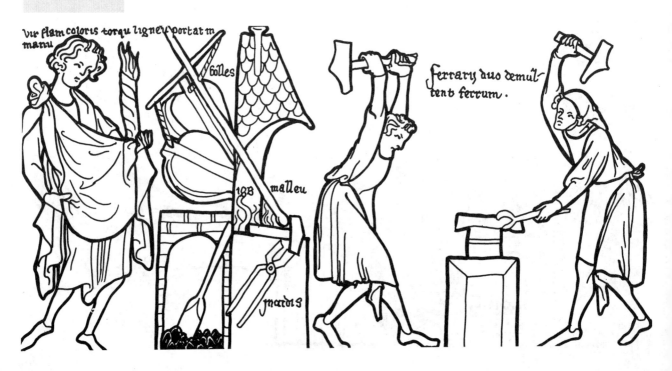

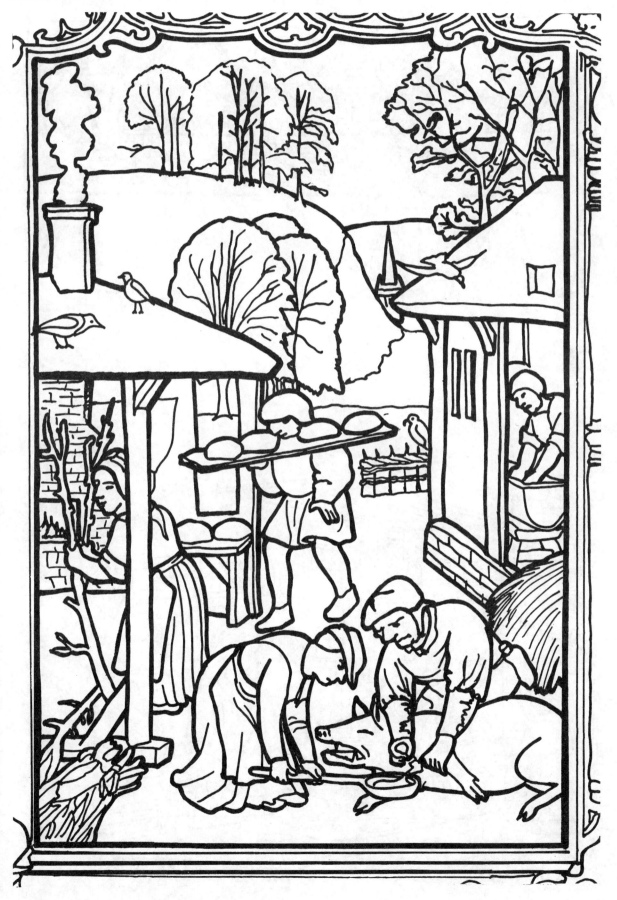

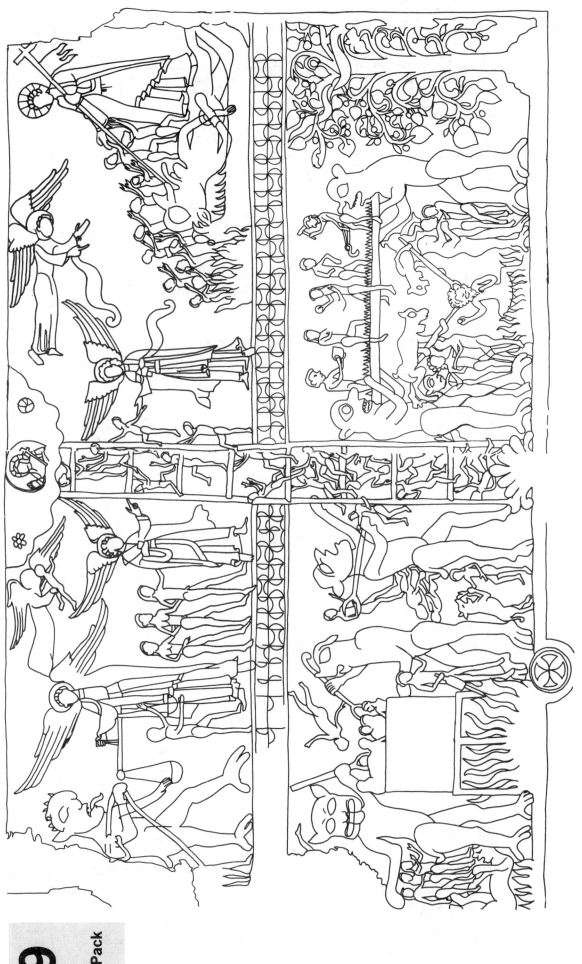

19

Picture Pack

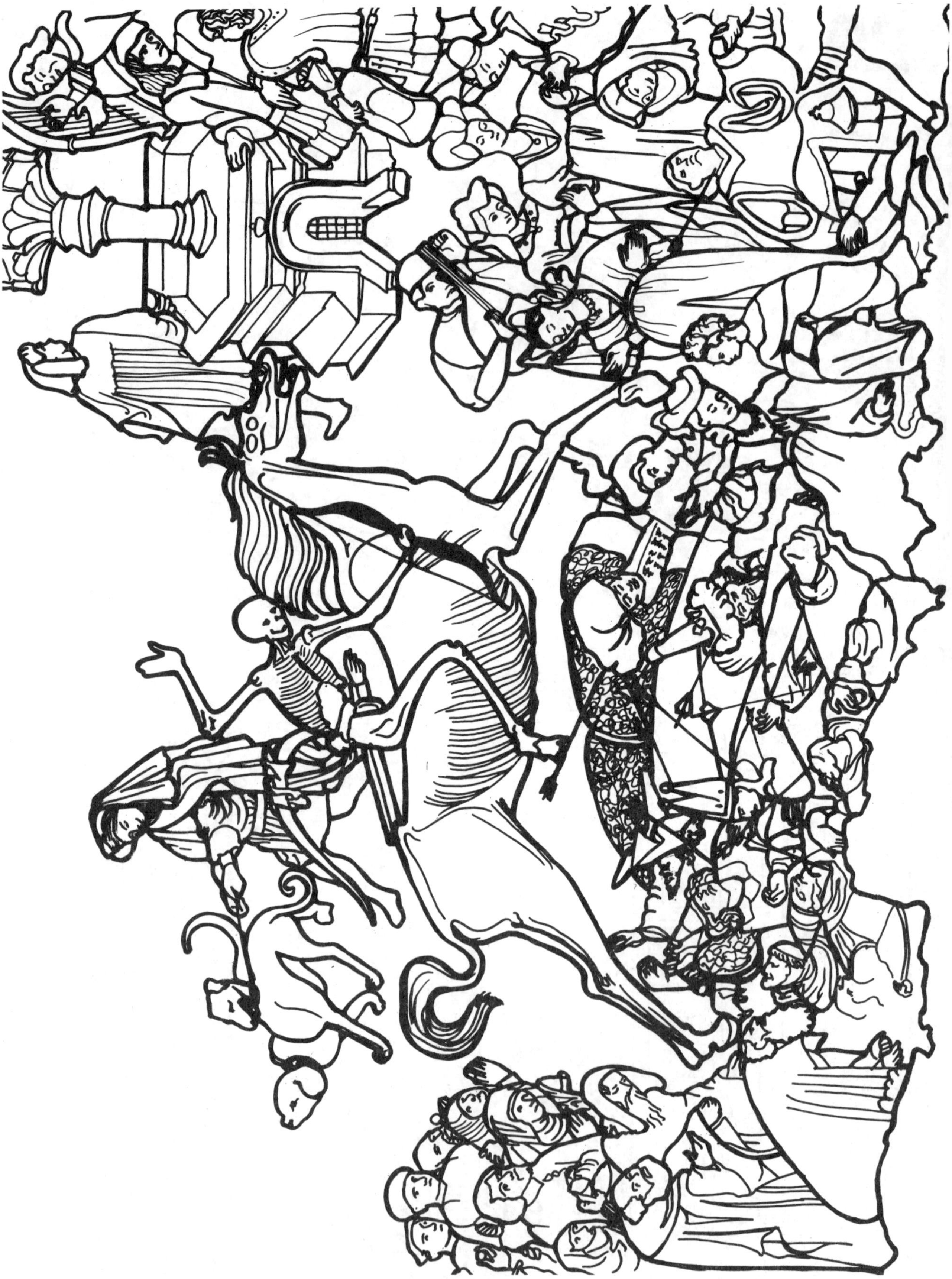

21

Picture Pack

MEDIEVAL REALMS SUPPORT MATERIALS